MW00876199

Draft2Digital Edition

Draft2Digital Edition License Notes

Dedication

Dedicated to my fiancé Tiffany. Thank you for all the support and encouragement you have given me.

Disclaimer:

This book is _not_ intended as advice. Please be advised: you are 100% responsible for all trades made in penny stocks, or any stocks in the stock market, and you should seek professional investment assistance before trading even a penny in the stock market. When investing, especially in penny stocks, you should be fully prepared to lose _everything_! The characters and events in this book are 100% real, although some of the book's features are enhanced for reading pleasure and the names of included persons and their respective associations are changed to protect their privacy.

By reading any further, you release the author and any connections to him or the book from any obligations or liabilities to your own trading, and furthermore, you agree not to bring any legal action against the author or any connections to him or the book for any losses incurred from your own trading or anyone who trades on your behalf or from any advice given by you based on this book.

Table of Contents

If you have any questions or need clarification, connect with the Author on Twitter: @AuthJB

Please leave a review if you find value in this book. A positive review is a great help to authors and we really

do appreciate our readers and any positive effects we have on you. Thank you and I truly hope you enjoy reading this book as much as I enjoyed writing it.

Introduction

Finding a bottomed out stock is easy. Finding a bottomed out stock that is about to turn back up north is hard. And entering that bottomed out stock at the correct price is the hardest part about bottom feeding. Just because the chart shows that the stock is bottomed, that doesn't mean that it will make the move back north in a timely manner or even at all. I have seen so many stock charts show that a particular company is way oversold only to have it continue to sell. The art is to find where the selling will stop and to enter the stock at that price or one tick above.

I am writing this book to help you develop the ability to discover where the selling will stop. It has taken me many painful years and a lot of money to finally get a system down that allows me to consistently buy a stock at the bottom. However, I'm still hashing out my ability to sell at the top. I tend to sell too early. And although I do make very decent gains (50%+), I sometimes miss a good 40%+ on most trades.

I'm not complaining though. For, in the penny world, as long as I am not losing money, I am happy. Penny stock trading is cut throat and it can quickly bleed your account. I learned this the hard way. There wasn't anything mainstream about penny stock trading when I first started out. There were a few YouTube videos, a couple of message boards, and a bunch of pumpers looking to make money off of newbie traders. I don't want what happened to me to happen to you.

By the time you finish reading "The Art of Bottom Feeding", you will have the knowledge to develop an uncanny ability to catch dropping stock prices at its bottom. This book is just your knowledge foundation. You still need to discover your own trading style and how to apply this knowledge to that style.

By catching a stock at the bottom, you will be one step ahead of the crowd and your account will grow faster than ever before. There really is an art to bottom feeding and a science. I have done the science part for you and I have developed it into an art. Now I give that art to you. The art consists of technical analyses while reading charts, financial and CEO research techniques to make sure your trade is safe, how to value a company to see if the true value is more than what it is selling at, and many more!

Read "The Art of Bottom Feeding" in its entirety. I have sprinkled in many extra bonuses throughout the chapters and, at the end of the book, I will give you many bonus chapters including chapters from my other penny stock books.

Here is the ticker symbol MINE chart that shows the power of catching the stock at the bottom and how much it can run. There's still a lot more room for MINE to increase in price.

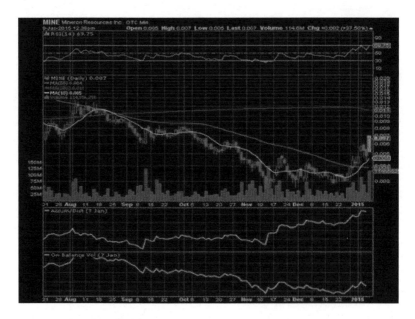

This chart has all the technical indicators that you will need to catch a stock at the bottom. These are the On Balance Volume line, the Accumulation and Distribution line, the ten day moving average, the fifty day moving average, the 200 day moving average (I often replace this with the Parabolic SAR if there is no impending cross present), the volume bars, and the relative strength index. Remember though, the chart is not the only thing that you need to look at. However, it is a very good starting point. When I am looking for a stock that has bottomed out, my first look is at the chart. Then I move on to the other information. We will come back to this chart again.

But for now, we will move on to the first and most powerful indictor to use to determine if a chart is bottomed, the On Balance Volume (OBV) line.

**NOTE: All charts, unless indicated, are looking at the daily timeframe.

Chapter 1 – Momentum Indicators

OBV Line

The On Balance Volume (OBV) line was developed by Joe Granville and is used to help predict the direction of the market. The OBV line measures the flow of volume. For instance, when the price closes higher than the previous day's close, the volume is added to the OBV line in an up direction. However, if the price closes lower than the previous day's close, the volume is added to the OBV line in a down direction. The OBV line is a single line that is generally shown on the bottom of the chart. When this line is bottomed out, it shows that the chart is oversold. This is a great indicator that the ticker price is bottomed. Additionally, when there's a small price increase but a large volume increase, the OBV line will move in a much sharper incline direction indicating that the price will increase. Therefore, a move in the upward direction of the OBV can serve as confirmation that the price will move higher. However, to get the full breadth of the move, assuming that all other due diligence indicates an upward move of the stock price, it is better to buy in before the positive move of the OBV. Buying before confirmation, also known as speculation, is risky. But with this risk comes the greatest reward. And that is what the art of bottom feeding is all about; the greatest reward!

Here is a great way to set up a stock chart:

On the bottom part of the screenshot in the "Indicators" section, you will see the OBV line (see the blue arrow). Generally, it's a good idea to leave the parameters blank on the OBV section.

The OBV line tends to predict what the price will do. It will usually shift before the price reacts. And volume is the major driving force behind the price of the stock. If there is a lot of selling volume, the price will decrease. If there is a lot of buying volume, the price will increase.

Let's look at the MINE chart again:

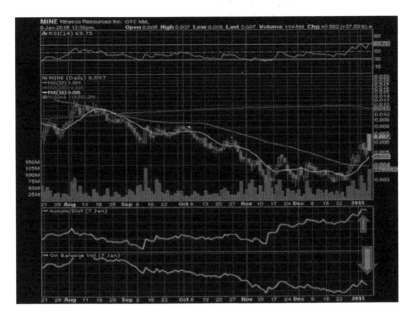

We see, as indicated by the blue arrows, that the accumulation distribution line is still going up but the OBV line is staying low. The OBV line is telling us that the price is going to come down some more. That is understandable because look how much MINE has climbed in the last two weeks. It's up over 100%. At this point, if I were to trade MINE, I would enter my bid price at the ten day moving average and just wait.

Now look at the accumulation distribution line. The increase in this line is showing that people are buying and holding, however, the tail end of the AD line is starting to turn south. It is indicating that traders are starting to take some profit off of the table. However, an uptrend is clearly forming and the low OBV indicates that the price has a lot of room to climb.

In "Penny Stock Players", one of the rules I mentioned was that price has a memory. That being said, if MINE breaks through the resistance of .008, as indicated by the two tops that formed in mid-September and early October (the dreaded bearish double top), then MINE can easily run to .014 as indicated by the share price high in August, with little resistance.

If a trader bought the low of .003 in mid-November, which a bottom feeder would have as indicated by the bottomed out OBV line, then the trader would be up 100% and could possibly see a profit of almost 500%! That is five times his or her money or $5,000.00 on a $1,000.00 investment in less than a year, as predicted by the chart. Of course, the chart would have to continue its uptrend to realize these gains. And in the penny stock world, anything is possible. Therefore, it is a good idea to take profits on the way up. For example, the trader could sell half of his or her position at 100% to remove his or her original position of $1,000.00 and then ride free shares for as long as he or she would like.

Additionally, to verify what we spoke about earlier about how a sharp increase in the OBV line indicates and is confirmation of an upward move in the price of the stock, look at the MINE chart around November 13th. You will see the sharp increase in the OBV line, a huge volume spike, and then an increase in price in four of the next five days. That is text book OBV line trading.

Now, you may look at the chart in mid-September and say, "Hey, the OBV line made a sharp upturn there too and I don't see an increase in price in the subsequent days, what gives?" And to this, I say look at the price action on the specific day in question. The price shot up like a bottle rocket, fizzing out just as quickly too. If the price moves on the same day as the OBV, the predictive value decreases. Additionally, look where the OBV line is during that time. It is high and is telling you that the stock is still overbought. With that being said, there are bound to be traders taking profits at these price levels. In order to buy the bottom of the stock, even if you are waiting for the confirmation of a sharp increase in the OBV line, that same line must first be bottomed out indicating that the stock is oversold as was the case in mid-November.

Minimize Risk: Buy when the OBV line begins to bounce up from the bottom.

AD Line

Now let's talk some about the Accumulation Distribution (AD) line, (see green arrow).

The AD line, much like the OBV line, is also a momentum indicator. However, it does this by determining whether or not traders are accumulating a stock or distributing a stock; that is to say, buying or selling a stock. Unlike the OBV line which predicts the direction of the stock, the AD line tells you exactly what's going on at this point in time. Are traders buying the stock or selling the stock? This is why you often see the two indictors moving in opposite directions. There is an exception to this rule. When there is divergence, which means when the AD line is moving in the opposite direction as its coinciding price, then the AD line predicts that the price will reverse its direction.

The OBV and AD lines are similar in that they take into account the volume of the stock. However, how they calculate the volume is different. Simply put, the OBV line adds the positive and negative volume together to create the line, taking into account the previous day's volume. So a huge volume day with a price close lower than the previous day, assuming you were using a daily timeframe on your chart, would cause the OBV line to decline. The AD line takes into account the close of a specific period relative to the high and low of that same period and the volume. Therefore, if the price closed closer to the high of the day, again assuming you were using the daily time, the AD line would increase, the amount of which dependent on the volume, even if the price decreased from the previous day.

Here are some numbers to help you understand the OBV and AD lines better. Let's say a stock closed at $0.01 yesterday. And today it opened at $0.01 and closed at $0.015. And let's say the stock hit a low price of $0.008 and a high of $0.022. The OBV line would see that the stock closed at $0.01 yesterday and closed today at $0.014, up a difference of $0.004. Therefore, the OBV line would move in the up direction, its sharpness depending on volume and price difference between the two closes. However, the AD line would ignore yesterday's close. Instead, it would focus on today's price fluctuation. Today's price hit a low of $0.008, a high of $0.022 and closed at $0.014. The difference between the high and the close is $0.008 and the difference between the close and the low is $0.006. Therefore, the close price was nearest to the low of the day and, subsequently, the AD line would decrease.

These indicators also work on the weekly timeframe. But instead of calculating a timeframe of day(s), it would calculate a timeframe of week(s). Generally, a trader will focus on the daily timeframe for trades that are to be completed within days to weeks, and will focus on the weekly timeframe for trades that are to be completed in weeks to months. Additionally, a weekly timeframe chart can be used to confirm a trend that is indicated on the daily timeframe.

Now, let's take a look at the MINE chart again:

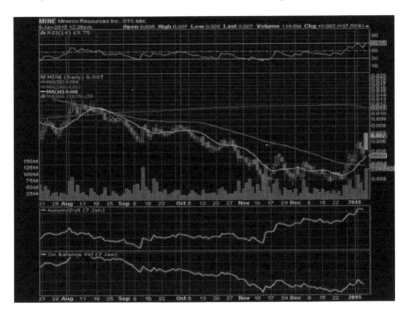

See in mid-November when the price dipped to its low of .003? The AD line then took a sharp turn north indicating that traders were accumulating the stock. There was also a ton of volume on that day. However, the price did not react positively for another two days. That is saying the AD line is also a futures predictor of price. If traders are buying and holding (accumulating), we know that the price has to react eventually. And if it hasn't yet, then that's a good indicator that we should be buyers the very next day, assuming the OBV is low, as it is in this case. After the AD line shifted and after the huge volume day, we still could've gotten .003 for two days if we set our bid and waited.

I mentioned before that right now, I'd put my bid in at the ten day moving average. However, when the ten day moving average is decreasing (curling down), I do not place my bid there. I bid lower.

Additionally, after the price spike in mid-November, the price mostly decreased until December 22nd. However, the AD line continued to steadily climb. Remember the divergence rule? The AD line was increasing while the price was decreasing indicating that the price will go up. And that's exactly what followed. The price subsequently increased after December 22nd and into 2015.

Here's FNMA's chart to further accentuate the power of these indicators:

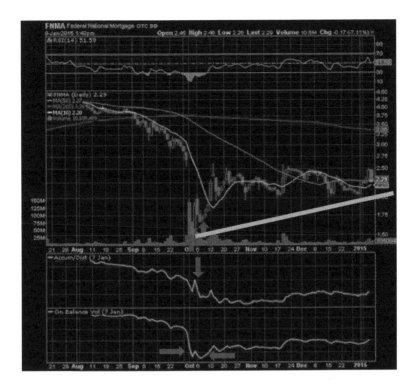

The above FNMA chart shows the OBV line has bottomed, the AD line took a sharp turn upwards, and because there were two OBV bottoms (double bottom), there were two solid entry points as indicated on the price section of the chart (see blue arrows). Additionally, FNMA is now on an uptrend but must stay above the tan trend line in order for the uptrend to continue, or at least to be confirmed that it will continue. Just because the price dips below that line does not mean the uptrend will have ended. It would just show the weakness of the uptrend. You could have made $1.00 a share profit from bottom feeding this trade, assuming that you sold.

Minimize Risk: Buy when the AD line and the price are in an upswing.

ADX Line with +DI and –DI

This and the following indicator was not mention in "Penny Stock Players" because The Student did not find it necessary for his style of trading. However, for the bottom feeder, these two indicators, while not completely crucial, can be game changers in a positive way.

The first indicator, the ADX or Average Direction Index, with positive and negative DMI (often denoted as +DI and –DI) or Directional Movement Indicators, shows the strength of the trend. For example, if the +DI line is above the –DI line, this denotes that prices are rising and the distance of the divergence specifies the strength of the positive movement. However, if the –DI is above the +DI, then this is indicating that the price is decreasing and, again, the distance of the divergence specifies the strength of the negative movement.

The distance of the divergence of the +DI and –DI is measured by the ADX line itself. Of course one could see the distance of divergence, however, having a line helps to quickly determine the strength of the trend, although it is not necessary. Therefore, this line, for all intents and purposes, could be ignored. The trader could then focus on the +DI and –DI lines exclusively.

However, if a trader chooses to use the ADX line, then the line will determine the strength of the trend in accordance to which DI line, positive or negative, is above the other. If the ADX line is moving in the down direction and the –DI is above the +DI, then although the chart is still in the negative direction (prices are decreasing), the downtrend is weakening. However, if the ADX line is increasing and the –DI is above the +DI, then the downtrend is increasing in strength and the chart will show that the stock is still heading further down in price.

The reverse is also true. If the ADX line is moving upwards and the +DI is above the –DI, then the chart is in an uptrend and increasing in strength.

The ADX line is on a scale from 0-100; the smaller the ADX number, the weaker the trend. Also, like the chart's price action as well as other indicators, when the line is either too high or too low, it will correct itself.

Let's take a look at a chart example of $VMGI's weekly chart:

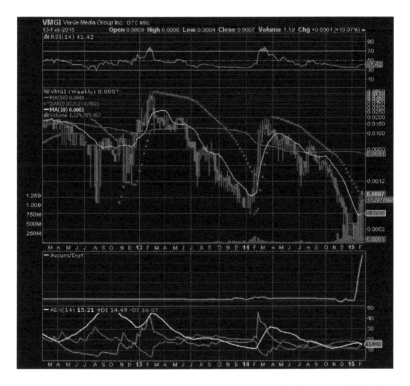

The ADX with +DI and –DI is the bottom indicator with the three lines crossing each other. As you can see, in mid-2012, $VMGI was in a major downtrend. The ADX line was off the chart! And the major divergence of the two DI lines is fairly significant. Then once the +DI crossed up through the –DI in late-2012, this was your buy signal and it denoted that the chart was trying to form an uptrend. However, before the cross, the ADX line reversed and started to head in the down direction indicating that the downtrend was losing steam.

Look further to the middle and late 2013 area of the chart and you will see that the –DI was above the +DI and the chart continued to decrease in price. But the ADX line (the line that appears the straightest of the three) was in a steady decline indicating that, although the price was decreasing, the downtrend was weakening.

Now look further still to the very right end of the chart. The +DI line is crossing up through the –DI. The price has already increased, however, the DI lines are currently giving the trader the buy signal. As it is commonly said in the OTC, volume comes before price. Check out the volume. It has increased for three straight days in the positive direction. But beware of the three day pump and dump and the final candle that was formed (candles will be described in more detail later).

Every time the +DI cross up through the –DI, the price increased substantially. The DI lines are indicating that this is about to happen again. And because the company is trading as such low prices, closed currently at .0007 a share, there is not much more room for a downtrend to continue. But every downtick in price comes with a heavier percentage decrease at these price levels. So beware.

Here is an annotated chart as a visual aid for what I have just described:

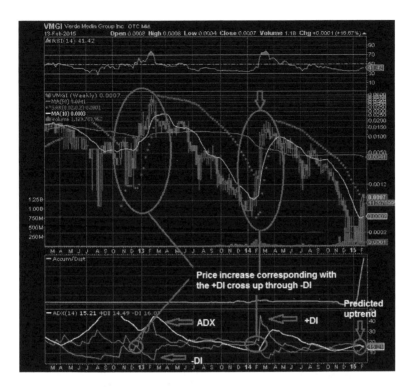

I cannot show this chart without also stating that the ADX line itself is still low, and curling down, indicating that the current few week uptrend is weak at the moment. But as we will discover in subsequent chapters, with all other indicators pointing to an uptrend formation, an entry here would most likely prove fruitful.

Minimize Risk: Buy when the ADX line is curling up and when the +DI is crossing up through the –DI.

We will now discuss the final indicator in this chapter.

Parabolic SAR

This indicator is often denoted as PSAR or SAR. It serves two functions. First, it shows the direction of the chart's momentum. And secondly, it shows reversal in that momentum relative to price.

If the SAR is above the chart, then the chart is in a downtrend, even if the price has recently increased. And if the SAR is below the chart, then the chart is in an uptrend, even if the price has recently decreased. Therefore, to confirm a reversal, a trader need only look at the location of the SAR. If recently the SAR was above the price bars on the chart and just switched to the bottom, the SAR then is telling the trader that the trend is reversing from bearish to bullish.

Here is $VMGI's chart again for this example:

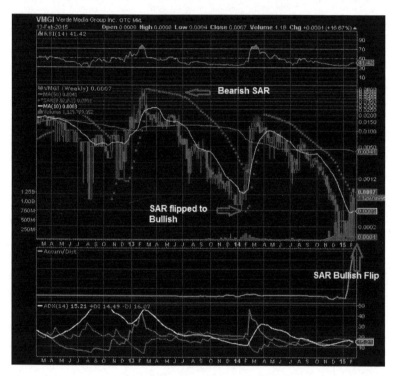

As you can see, when the SAR is above the price candles, the price keeps decreasing. And even though the price increased a few times during the downtrend, the SAR stayed above the price indicating the downtrend was still in effect. However, when the SAR is below the line, the uptrend becomes fully in effect.

One of the rules in "Penny Stock Players" is that bottoms take longer to form than tops. Look at the chart above. The bottom of the chart, before the bullish reversal, took a whole year to form in 2013. However, the top formed in a matter of 3 months in early 2014.

To the far right end of the chart, as with the DI lines, the SAR is indicating an uptrend formation due to it flipping to the bottom of the price candles from the top of the price candles. This chart is fully indicating a forming uptrend and a bullish takeover.

Minimize Risk: Buy when the PSAR flips to the bottom of the price bars.

Chapter 2 – Volume & Moving Averages

Volume drives price action in the stock world. However, very high volume that is sustained will stop any momentum in the stock. It does this because there will eventually be just as many people selling as there are buying. In this case, the stock will trade sideways. In other words, there will be little price action until the bulls or the bears take over.

Initially though, you want volume in a stock. This is especially true if you are trying to catch a pump and dump. However, if you are trying to catch the bottom as a bottom feeder, you want to buy before the volume hits. If you wait until the volume comes into the stock and everyone else starts trading it, you may miss a huge chunk of profits. Penny stocks are very volatile and can actually move on low or average volume. But it must be a historically very slow trading stock. Sometimes you can catch gems like that. And once everyone else gets wind of this gem, volume will hit it like a hurricane and you would be smart to take profits based on your system.

The ten day moving average is an excellent trend indicator. It closely follows the price and can alert you when a trend is reversing. If you see the ten day moving average shift down, the stock will most likely start a down trend and vice versa.

Here's a chart that exemplifies the 3 most powerful indicators (the OBV line, the 10 day moving average, and volume). VDRM's 3 month chart:

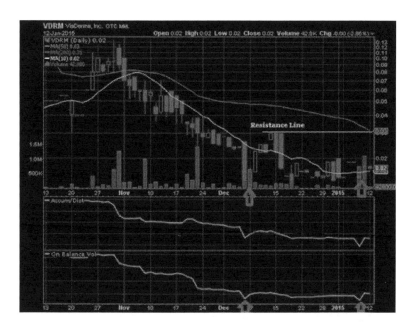

This chart in and of itself is perfect for a bottom feed trade. Remember though, there are other factors which we will discuss later that must also be taken into account. But for a chart, you do not get much better than that!

First, let's take a look at the OBV line. See how it has fallen along with the price? Then we have the dip in the OBV line that coincides with the bottom of the price dip (see the first set of blue arrows on the price section of the chart and on the OBV line, reading left to right). Once you saw the OBV line dip, that was your key to enter. If you bought there, we will have to estimate that the price was near a penny because it isn't shown on the chart. However, it is one hundred percent clear that the price was under two cents.

Next, look at the volume that coincides with the price. It is more than double the previous day, which is more than double the day before. And the volume on the day in question is so high that it swallows the price bar. The price action follows the volume action and the price did just that. It increased for the next three days before traders took profits. Then immediately following the first red bar after the first blue arrow the price gapped up. A gap up is when the price opens higher than where it closed on the previous day. A gap down is when the price opens lower than where it closed on the previous day.

The gap up triggered sellers to sell and the price fell back down. That's a clear pump and dump, although very short in duration. We call this "closing the gap", when the price gaps up and then the price comes back down to the previous day's close. This sometimes takes multiple days to complete but must happen before the price continues upward.

Now look at the tan horizontal resistance line that I've drawn for you on the chart. The price hit three cents before it came back down. Let's say, for this example, you bought at a penny and a half when you saw the dip in the OBV line. You just made close to 100% on your trade by realizing this was a pump and dump and selling on the third day at almost three cents, as I outlined in my previous book, "Market Manipulation".

In my first book, "Penny Stock Players", I outlined a set of rules to use for trading. One of those rules is that price has a memory. Let's take a look now at the second set of blue arrows. As you can see, the OBV has bottomed again. The price didn't dip as much but it is still a good time to enter. Furthermore, because the low is higher than the previous low and that low is higher than the low before that, there is a potential uptrend in the making. Additionally, notice that the ten day moving average (the white line that is following the price action on the above chart) has recently shifted positive. It's not a sharp upward movement, but it is positive nonetheless. This is another indicator that an uptrend is in the making. The opposite of an uptrend is what you see on the chart in early November. The ten day moving average shifted down indicating that a downtrend was virtually imminent. The price confirmed this indicator.

Remember the rule about price having a memory? This new pump can and probably will run to three cents as long as all of the indicators prove true. Nothing in the penny stock world is set in stone and it is easy to get faked out here. But based on the chart alone, this is a great bottom feeder's trade again. The OBV dipped, the volume was great on the entry day, the ten day moving average has shifted back positive, and the price is slowly rising.

In my experience, the slow rising price has more potential to net you higher gains because the volume increase is steadier and so the stock's momentum doesn't fizz out so fast. But even in this case, it is still smart to take profits according to your system.

Here's another nugget for the ten day moving average. One of the most bullish signs on a chart is when the volume is high and the ten day moving average crosses up through the fifty day moving average (the blue line that is following the price action on the above chart). Traders like to call the fifty day moving average moving up through the two hundred day moving average a golden cross because of its bullish indication. However, I have found that the ten day moving up through the fifty day is a much more truthful cross and, because the averages are closer together and are affected by price much more readily due to their limited time frame, it is much easier to trade.

If you look at the above chart, you will see that the ten day moving average has not only begun to curl up positive, but it is also closing in on the fifty day moving average for the cross. The cross didn't quite happen during the earlier pump. The moving averages barely touched.

It is worth it to note that the cross is a lagging indicator, meaning that the price will not react immediately. The time frame from the cross to the price increase, if there is one, is subject to the chart and the way traders trade the stock. Volume plays a huge role here. So do not buy a stock just because you see a cross. Make sure you cross check it with all of the other indicators first.

Wow, you are in for a treat on this day. I am so glad that I was able to write this book at this time so I can show you how these indicators work in as real time as I can. Remember the chart earlier of the stock with the symbol MINE in chapter 1? Well, here it is again four days later. And mind you, the cross had just happened a few days prior.

The three month MINE chart:

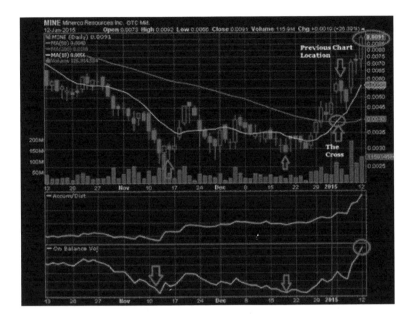

Again, the first two arrows are your entry points. The blue circle indicates "the cross" of the ten day moving average up through the fifty day moving average. I've indicated where the price was when I first posted this chart. The price has climbed another 50% since the cross. In total, if you bought at the second blue arrow at a price of $.003 and sold on January 12, 2015 at $.009, then you just made 200%, or $2,000.00 profit on a $1,000.00 investment, in less than a month.

On the chart, I circled the current price with red and the current location of the OBV line in red to indicate that it is time to sell this stock. It may continue to rise. Heck, you can get 1,000% out of this stock. But smart money takes profits and, at this time, the stock is overbought and profits should be taken.

Also, take a note of the giant volume bar on January 10th and the volume bar on the day that coincided with the cross, which is twice the size as the previous day. What a perfect chart that traded exactly the way it was supposed to, which isn't always the case.

In fact, let's take a look at a chart that didn't exactly act accordingly.

Here is the six month chart of ticker symbol SHOM:

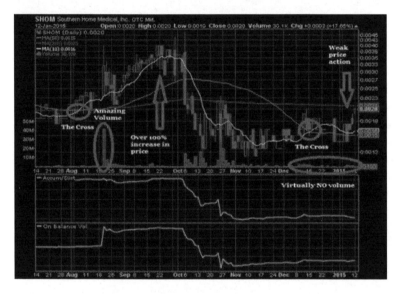

The SHOM chart shows that the cross, along with the volume, proved to be a bullish indicator and the price reacted accordingly. The volume did not come in on SHOM on the day of the cross. But, like I mentioned earlier, the cross is a lagging indicator. However, the second time the cross hit, there has been virtually no volume, and so the price, although increased a little, never gained full steam. I should also mention that when the ten day moving average crosses down into the fifty day moving average, it is considered bearish and indicates that the price is going to decrease. This is also shown on the chart above.

The above SHOM chart, if I was bottom feeding, would've afforded me only one buying opportunity. That trade would have come on October 26th. The price would have been between $0.0013 and $0.0014. Assuming I got the latter price, I would have set my sell at $0.0021. That means I'd still be holding my shares. However, I would have been real tempted to lower my sell price to $0.002 so I could have gotten out today. But in reality, I never made this trade.

***NOTE: The reason the lower moving average cross up through a higher moving average is bullish is because it shows that traders are paying more for the stock in recent days than they have been in the more distant past.

Minimize Risk: Buy when a smaller moving average crosses up through a larger moving average and is accompanied by increasing volume.

Chapter 3 – RSI Indicator & Candles

The relative strength index (RSI) deserves a chapter by itself. Although it is the author's choice to spot trades based on the OBV line, it is no secret that the RSI is probably the most commonly used indicator when determining whether or not a stock is overbought or oversold. But when combing the RSI with the OBV, you will be unstoppable.

Before we get into the RSI, let's take a look at the MINE charts as it stands today:

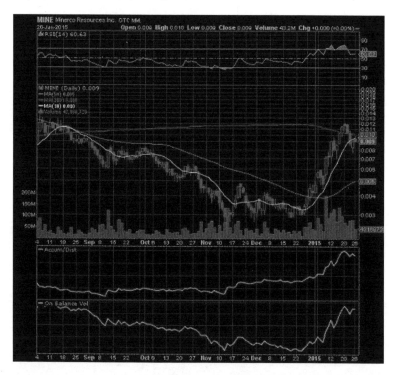

This chart has all the indicators (RSI, OBV, AD, Volume, Price, 10 day MA, 50 day MA, 200 day MA). If you remember from before, I would have sold MINE around the $0.0091 price. That would have meant that I would have missed out on another $0.0029 in gains, which is fine by me. I'd rather be safe than sorry. Remember, when pigs become hogs they get slaughtered. Do not be greedy or you will get burned. Keep true to your rules and guidelines and trade accordingly and do not get upset if you miss gains that you could have had. Any gain is better than a loss. However, with MINE, one can clearly see an uptrend forming. So this might not be a bad set it and forget it long term trade or investment. But that is not the discussion of this book.

The RSI helps the trader determine if the stock is overbought or oversold by comparing the magnitude of gains versus the magnitude of losses in a given time range. The formula is: $[100 - 100 / (1 + RS)]$. RS is the average number of up closes divided by the average number of down closes.

The RSI ranges from 0 to 100. Generally, it is observed that an RSI at 70 or above is overbought and an RSI of 30 or below is oversold. Look at the MINE chart above to see this in action. The RSI fell below 30 at the exact point where you should have bought and hit above 70 twice, once at the $.0091 price that I said I would have sold, and also at its current price. MINE, at its current price, is overbought and should see a decline in price in the short term.

In "Penny Stock Players", the Student did not use the RSI much. But he was more interested in riding momentum on a stock that has already turned around and bounced off of the floor into an upward swing. However, when bottom feeding, the RSI is critical. Of course, you do not have to wait for the RSI to reach 30 or below. This is because although you may be missing out on potential gains by buying a stock a little higher than you'd like, you are also maximizing your chances of buying an oversold stock because not all stocks reach an RSI of 30 or below before they turn around.

Make no mistake, a chart set up with price that has steadily declined for a few weeks to months, a bottomed OBV line that has sharply turned north (but still very low), high volume, little to no price action, an AD line that is steadily rising, an up curling 10 day MA with a potential 50 day MA cross, a PSAR that's flipped to the bottom, and an RSI under 30 is, by far, the most explosive chart set up that you could possibly imagine and can help you realize gains that you have never seen before. However, there is still the aspect of news and press releases that could make or break even the best of charts.

***NOTE: It is generally accepted that an RSI under 50 is sold enough for a buy in. As I mentioned above, the RSI should fall to 30 or around 30 for a confirmation that the ticker is oversold. However, an RSI under 50, especially if the stock is in an uptrend, is well enough. Again, develop your own style and remember, depending on the pattern of the chart, the RSI will present different each time. In that sense, a stock chart in a downtrend may hit an RSI under 30. However, a stock chart in an uptrend may never even fall to an RSI of 40. It's all in the pattern and the history of the chart, as well as your own style of trading.

Let's review another chart. The following is the chart for the ticker symbol IJJP:

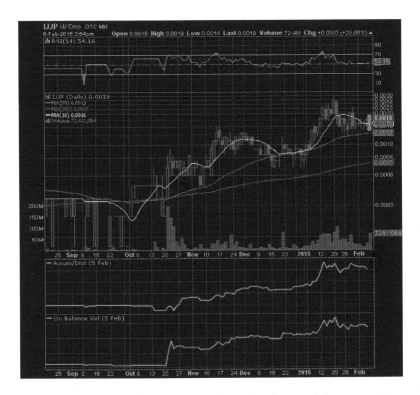

The chart was so choppy before the huge volume spike after October 20, 2014 that it would not have proven to be a good trade. However, that volume spike pushed the price up dramatically. Then a series of flag patterns followed as the price continued to climb. The price would rise substantially, then a period of consolidation followed as bears began to take profits. Then the bulls would return and the price would rise again. This has happened three times and I predict that a fourth could be on the horizon.

Remember the golden crosses? The 10 day moving average moved up through the 50 day moving average AND the 50 day moving average moved up through the 200 day moving average. Smart traders usually wait for confirmation before buying in, even if they are bottom feeding. Why? Because although a stock that is bottomed out *can* rise, there is no guarantee that it will, even if the chart is set up perfectly. And if it doesn't, then the trader would have to stay in this ticker for as long as it takes for it to prove true. Or the trader would have to sell the ticker for break even or for a loss.

Let's look at the chart again in annotated fashion:

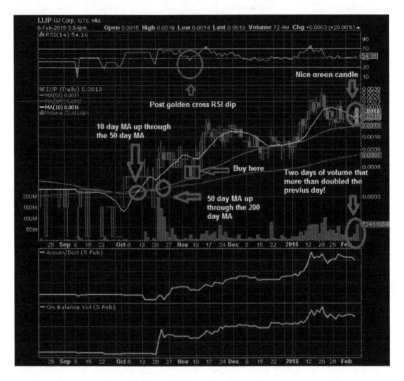

IJJP is in an uptrend. Once that huge volume spike hit after October 20, 2014, there were three flag-like patterns showing a bullish upward movement followed by a bearish consolidation. Therefore, since IJJP is in an uptrend, if you look at the RSI, it never hit 30. However, the RSI did dip below 50, which would have been your confirmation of the buy signal caused by the volume spike. The RSI actually dipped below 50 twice after the 10 day MA move up through the 50 day MA.

So what's the point? If you did not buy in on the huge volume spike day due to fear that you saw it too late and the price increased too much, the following RSI dip below 50 would have been your next buy signal with a buy in price of $0.0006 as indicated by the "Buy here" annotation on the chart. Funny thing is, the price would still have been $0.0006. Once you learn them, trust the indicators!

If you bought at $0.0006 as those indicators told you to, you would be sitting at $0.0018 for three times your money as of February 06, 2015. So you just turned $300 into $900 or $3000 into $9000 depending on your own risk management system.

But this chart is *not* done yet! The volume has picked back up and the candle has turned green and with a double wick, closing closer to the top of the wick. Looks like IJJP is ready to push up to new highs. Remember, to buy in at support.

Let's look at the chart again to see what price would indicate support:

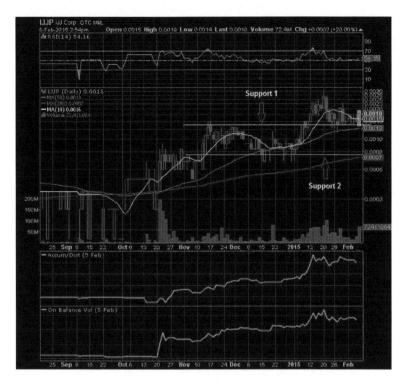

Support, as defined as a price that the ticker has dipped to but has bounced up from, on IJJP is currently at $0.0014 as indicated by the top yellow line (Support 1). However, if that would fail, the next support price would be all the way down at $0.0008. Again, this trade comes down to risk management and trust. How strongly do you feel that the first support level will hold? The price has hit $0.0014 twice and bounced off of it both times. To me, it seems strong enough, especially since the chart is in such an uptrend. However, you have to decide for yourself and trade accordingly.

Additionally, if you bought IJJP way down at $0.0006 and are holding, although a smarter way will be divulged in the next chapter, you would hold unless the first support level at $0.0014 did not hold up. A sell at $0.0014 for over 200% is safer than holding once support fails. Not selling at these high price percentage gains is face slapping territory. So be smart!

***NOTE: The OBV is no longer bottomed in this chart. However, remember, indicators should be used in conjunction with each other and never by themselves. Since all other indicators suggest a positive move in price, the OBV line can be trumped, and the ticker can still be a good buy.

In "Penny Stock Players", I did not mention much about candles. But if you are going to play the bottom of the chart and try to catch it perfectly, you need to know candles! So...what is a candle exactly? It is just the price action for a current day or a current week. Most of the above charts are of the daily time frame. Therefore, a candle will show at what price the stock was at when it was at the low of the day, the high of the day, and where the price opened and closed.

The wide part of the candle shows where the price opened and closed and the skinny parts of the candle shows where the price hit, either high or low, but could not hold. A red candle denotes a trade day where the ticker closed at a price lower than where it opened. And a green candle denotes a trade day where the ticker closed at a price higher than where it opened.

Here is an up close picture of a few candles:

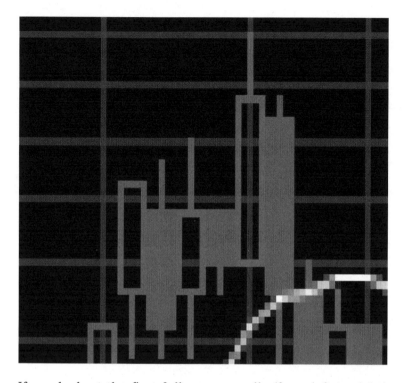

If you look at the first full green candle (from left to right), you will see that the price closed at the top of the candle. However, it did hit at a price lower than the open. The wide part of the candle shows the open and close and the skinny part hanging from the bottom sows where the price hit when it was at its lowest for the day. The next candle, a red one, shows that the price opened at the top of the wide part and closed at the bottom of the wide part. However, the stock hit a price higher than it opened and lower than it closed, which is why you have two skinny parts sticking out on the top and the bottom. That is how candles are formed and each type of candle is read by chartists as a signal to buy, sell, or hold.

Here is the same candle chart but annotated:

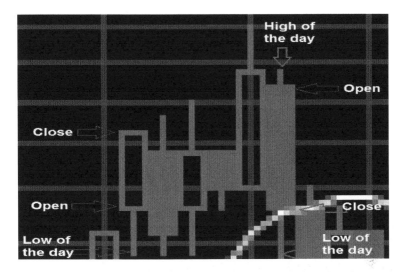

There are four very bullish candles that indicate the reversal of a downtrend that you can use to catch the bottom of a chart. These four candles are bullish engulfing, the doji star, the hammer, and the inverted hammer. These candles are only bullish if they occur during a downtrend or consolidation. If they occur at the top of an uptrend then they could indicate a trend reversal to the downside.

In the picture above, the third full green candle shows bullish engulfing. This is when the price at least doubles the previous day and is green (closes higher than it opened). Here's an annotated picture of bullish engulfing:

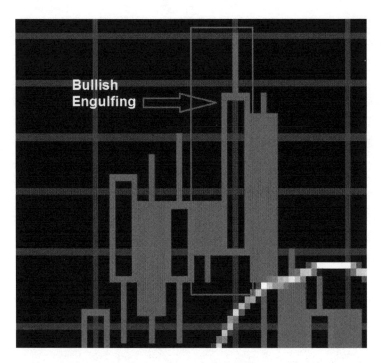

Here is a picture of an inverted hammer:

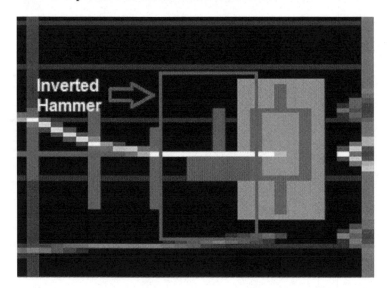

The hammer is the same as the inverted hammer except the wide part of the candle is at the top and the skinny part of the candle (the hammer handle) is at the bottom.

And finally, here is a picture of the doji:

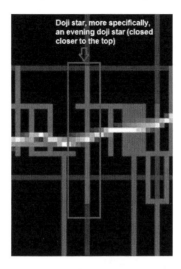

As with all other indicators, the candle on the chart should not be used alone. It should be used in conjunction with other technical analysis. These technical indicators include but are not limited to volume, moving averages, momentum indicators, and the candles. There are many other indicators that a trader can use, however, it is best to keep it simple. Too many indicators can become too confusing and can even stagnate your trading due to conflicting information.

Here is a real time example of the power of bullish engulfing with high volume. The following two charts are of $IJJP. The first is Friday, February 6, 2015 and the second is Monday, February 9, 2015.

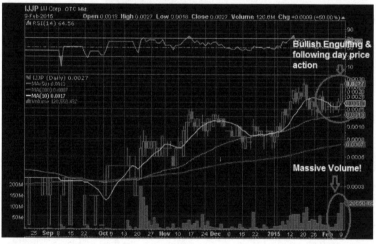

Here is the latter chart zoomed in on the time frame in question for emphasis:

Naturally, this stock is not bottomed out. However, it does show the proof of the power of bullish engulfing. Knowing how to read candles is a great skill to add to your repertoire of stock trading knowledge. Additionally, the red candle before the green bullish engulfing candle is an inverted hammer. That also, as previously mentioned, is a candle that signifies a reversal. And since is occurred during a consolidation period as the price slowly decreased, it denotes a bullish move upward in price. The bullish engulfing was your confirmation of a buy. And if you waited until the next day to buy $0.0018 and sold the next day at $0.0027, you would have realized 50% profit.

***NOTE: A Hammer that forms at the top of a current uptrend (and usually red indicating a lower close price than the open) is called a hanging man and is indicative of a bearish reversal into a downtrend. Also an inverted hammer at the top of an uptrend (and usually red indicating a lower close price than the open) is called a shooting star and is also indicative of a bearish reversal into a downtrend. Therefore, you want these hammers to form at the bottom of a downtrend and generally you want them to be green.

Minimize risk: Buy when RSI is below 50 (preferably at 30 or below) and when the chart shows a reversal candle followed by a confirmation candle.

Chapter 4 – The Indicators: Putting It All Together

In order to perfect the Art of Bottom Feeding, the trader must be proficient in chart reading. For this technique, the indicators we have learned are the On Balance Volume line, the Accumulation Distribution line, the ADX line with +DI and –DI, the Parabolic SAR, volume bars, moving averages (10 day, 50 day, and 200 day), the Relative Strength Index, and how to spot bullish candles (bullish engulfing, doji star, and the hammers).

The OBV, RSI, and AD lines show when the stock is overbought or oversold. The ADX line shows the strength of the trend. The DI lines show whether the stock is in an uptrend or downtrend. The Parabolic SAR shows the reversal of the trend. The candles also denote reversal or continuance patterns. And the volume indicates how many shares were traded on that day or week indicating the volatility of the stock. And for penny stocks, we want volatility because, without it, there's no price action and we do not make any money if there's no price action.

Let's analyze the $VMGI chart again here:

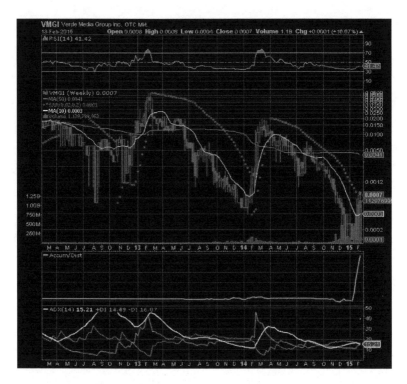

The RSI is below 50 indicating a buy signal. The parabolic SAR has flipped to the bottom of the price section of the chart indicating bullishness. There was a bullish engulfing followed by a green hammer (with the wick at the bottom of the candle and longer than the body). The bullish engulfing indicates bullishness but the green hammer at the top of the current increasing price bars is bearish. The volume has increased tremendously for three straight weeks and is green indicating bullish buying. The AD line has topped out indicating bullish accumulation. The +DI line is about to cross up through the –DI line indicating bullishness. The 10 day MA is curling up and heading towards the 50 day MA for a cross, also a bullish indication.

In fact, there are only two slightly bearish indicators and one strong bearish indicator on this chart. The ADX line is turned slightly down indicating that the strength of the uptrend is weakening and the ADX line is low, also indicating a weak trend. The hammer candle is the strong bearish indicator that we need to worry about. However, because the bullish uptrend is in its infancy compared to the bearish downtrend that it is trying to reverse out of, it may take some more buying power for these indicators to show an increase in the power of the pre-mature uptrend. All other indicators predict that the price will go higher and the pattern of the chart also predicts this.

Minimize risk: Make sure the indicators you use all line up for the trend you are trading. If one or more fail, do not make that trade.

Chapter 5 – The True Pump

We have all heard of the pump and dump, right? Well, in "Penny Stock Players" I wrote about the pump and dump and how to trade it. And in "Market Manipulation", I wrote about how traders use the pump and dump to manipulate the stock price.

However, in this book we will be taking a look at how a true pump works. There really isn't supposed to be a dump. The dump is for the manipulators and the traders who are out to steal your hard earned money. But that is not the topic of this book. And it is also not the intention of the "Penny Stock Players" series. Here, we try to help protect you from the dump. Therefore, the following is how the true pump is supposed to work and how, if traders would follow this simple rule, *everyone*, including the traders, the company, and the economy, would win.

The true pump is truly very simple and it works like this: First, you need enough traders to bring in enough volume to push the price up. So, if you trade with fellow traders who know what they are doing, which I recommend you do, then you all would buy into the same ticker. Remember though, you *all* buy in at support!

If there are a thousand traders buying into the same ticker and only a hundred were able to buy in at support, then that is fine. The price will increase and then those sellers will sell at resistance. Then a hundred more people, or even the same people who previously bought in at support, buys in at the new support. Sometimes this new support is at the same price as the initial support. However, for the true pump to work, this new support should be higher than the previous support *and* give new traders a confident buy-in price.

Now, we have two support levels at which traders were able to buy into the same ticker. Now everyone sells again at the next level of resistance and buys in again at the new support level. This could continue forever as the price of the stock continues to rise. And by doing this, there is no dump. Nobody loses their shirt and everyone makes profits as the stock price increases. The company also makes money through the traders as they buy the stock. And the economy benefits because we are dumping money back into society through the business *and* through our trade account via trade costs.

Sounds simple, huh? Well, in theory it is. We as traders can keep increasing the price indefinitely. It helps us and fellow traders, it helps the company, and it helps the economy. But why is it so difficult? Because it is hard to find traders who are willing to buy at support *and* sell at resistance. Eventually, some traders will get greedy and want to hold their shares for 1,000% gains and ultimately block any further increase in the share price thereby killing momentum and causing the price to plummet into the dump. Additionally, there comes a price range that traders consider too much to pay. Once this range hits, watch out for the bottom!

The IJJP chart shows a perfect true pump. The price increases, then traders sell at resistance causing the chart to consolidate. Then once consolidation is over, the traders buy back in at support and cause the price to increase again. Then another consolidation and chart reset (chart resetting is when an overbought ticker is sold until it is no longer overbought), etc...

Here is what happens when the pump fails:

The pump worked for three legs but then it lost steam and everyone dumped. This is an insane dump. The price fell all the way down to $0.0001. But this does not mean that it was completely caused by traders dumping their shares. The company could have issued millions or billions of more shares into their outstanding shares or float and destroyed their share structure. Nonetheless, the price crashed and now it is hardly traded. These types of charts should be avoided as they aren't worth trying to catch the bottom. If a trader wants to trade this, he or she should make sure all confirmation signals constitute a buy signal and wait for great news that causes the trading to turn back positive to hit the news feeds.

As of now though, the chart is so choppy and nasty that a good trader would avoid it. One should not be so quick to jump into a stock just because it has dropped all the way down to $0.0001. The risk far outweighs the benefits. A reverse split could be on the horizon here and *NO* trader wants to get caught in one of those!

On the flip side of a pump failure, is a pump success. But this pump does not necessarily occur just because traders are pushing the price up. The company could actually be bringing in massive revenue and paying off debt. And as the debt decreases, the company can retire shares and decrease the outstanding shares and, subsequently, decrease the float. By retiring shares and retaining the net positive cash, the price per share will increase.

Companies are graded on their net cash flow. However, in the penny stock world, this is not a viable option. Most penny stocks are, for lack of a better word, garbage. Most penny stocks have toxic debt, little to no revenue, and an atrocious share structure. With all this being said, they are almost impossible to evaluate based on value and financials. Nonetheless, reading financials, filings, press releases and news is an important aspect of penny stock trading. You can't trade based on the chart alone every time or you will get burned. There's an old saying in the penny stock world, "know what you own". And you can't know what you own if you do not do your full due diligence and research.

Most traders fail because of three main reasons. These reasons are because they do not do the work necessary to become successful, they do not have rules that govern their trading, or they do not observe their own rules.

Now, here's a chart of a true pump:

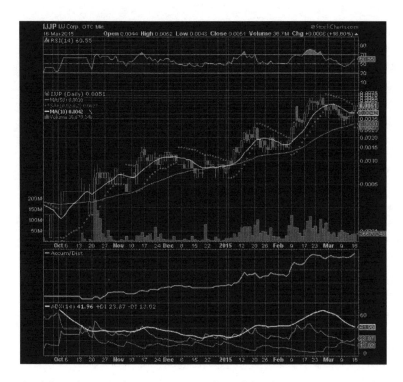

And here's one that got started and had some success but now looks as though it is failing:

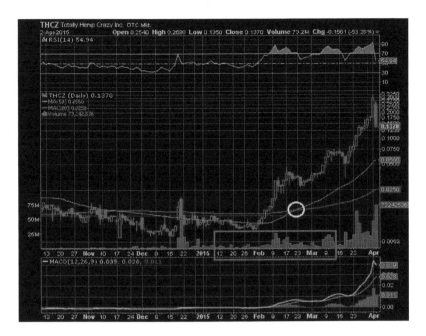

I deliberately left out most of the annotations so that you can practice discovering the patterns yourself.

Minimize risk: <u>Never</u> buy in on an uptrend until the chart shows consolidation and confirmation of the next leg of the pump.

Chapter 6 – Financials & Share Structure

Financials

Yes, we are going to talk about the dreaded financial analysis of stocks. This is where we get down and dirty. Traders must become proficient in reading financials, researching the CEO, determining how well the share structure is set up, and how to interpret news, which is often cryptic to the untrained eye.

Let's start by getting the financials out of the way since they are the driest subject and the most tedious research that traders have to deal with. We will start with some elementary basics and definitions. If you look at the balance sheet, which can be found on many websites, but two very good websites are yahoo finance and OTC markets, you will see a bunch of numbers in columns under headings by year.

***NOTE: You can find the balance sheet on the left column of yahoo finance on a stock ticker page under the "Financials" heading. Likewise, you can find it on OTCMarkets.com under the "Financials" heading on the left column of the stock ticker page.

These numbers coincide with income, debt, total liabilities, total assets and the like. Go ahead and take a look quickly at a balance sheet in the finance section of a company's yahoo finance profile. For simplicity's sake, we will take a look at three companies. One, a blue chip company called Disney with the stock ticker symbol: DIS. Another company is a penny stock with the ticker symbol: NSAV. And finally, ticker symbol: FNMA, a penny stock company defined as any stock trading under $5.00 a share. Pink sheets and over the counter stocks are those that are not trading in a major stock exchange. FNMA is currently trading in the mid $2.00 range and as an OTCBB company.

But before we look those up, here are a few quick definitions and tips. First, a negative number will be in parenthesis instead of having a dash in front of it. For example, -29 will be written as (29). Furthermore, the numbers are represented as 1,000s of dollars as indicated in the upper right hand corner of any balance sheet. So a (29) would be a debt of $29,000 or also known as a -$29,000 balance.

The balance sheet often has three sections: assets, liabilities, and stock holder equity. Assets are the actually money income that the company itself generates mainly by either selling goods and services or investing, and any value of land, building, machinery and equipment. Liabilities represent mainly debt, payroll and cash taken out of the business for materials and equipment purchases. And stock holder equity is the money flow that comes to the company via stock holders who buy their stock.

If you look at the balance sheet of NSAV, you will quickly see, at the bottom of the page in the "Net Tangible Assets" category a negative balance in parentheses. If you look further up in the total assets section, you will see that it is significantly lower than the total liability amount and thus, the net tangible assets is negative and the stock of the price is in the triple digits to the right of the zero, or $0.0002 as of February 2015.

Furthermore, if you look at the net total assets again, you will see that the number has actually decreases year by year. This is the complete opposite of what you should be looking for. Of course most of these penny stock companies are going to have low numbers here, even negative numbers. However, you want to see the numbers becoming more positive over time, not more negative over time.

So are there any positives for this company? Let's look at NSAV's cash flow statement to find out...

The cash flow statement is slightly more positive. The net income in all three posted years is negative. However, the number keeps becoming more positive each year meaning that they are increasing their income each year. The same can be said for the total cash flow for operating expenses.

Of course, in the case of NSAV, there could be other factors that would entice you to buy into this stock at such a low price of $0.0002. Based on financials, NSAV looks to be trying to pay off some of its debt, however, in doing so, it is also losing total asset value year by year.

Before we analyze what all this means towards our decision to purchase shares of NSAV, let's take a look at Disney and see what their balance sheet and cash flow looks like.

Disney has total assets of $84 billion, liabilities of $39 billion, stock holder equity of $44 billion and net tangible asset total of $9 billion. In its cash flow statement, Disney discloses that it has $9.7 billion dollars in total cash flow from operating activities, compared to the negative numbers in NSAV. And finally, Disney has a total cash flow from financing activities of negative $6.7 billion dollars.

All of these numbers are provided for free at yahoo finance and OTC markets websites. But, as we can see, there is a stark difference between a booming blue chip company

(Disney) and a penny stock company that does not seem like they are going to be around much longer.

Finally, for financials, let's take a look at FNMA. On the balance sheet, FNMA has total assets of $3.27 trillion dollars, total liabilities of $3.26 trillion dollars, and total shareholder equity of $9.5 billion dollars, which is the same dollar figure of their net tangible assets. FNMA's cash flow statement shows a total operating activity cash flow of $12.9 billion dollars, a total cash flow from financing activities of negative $467 billion dollars.

Everything looks good for FNMA except one thing. First, it looks like two things as the total assets is 0.01 trillion dollars more than its total liabilities. But before we assume that's not a lot of money, let's remember we are talking in trillions of dollars. So, in reality, the assets are ten billion dollars more than the liabilities. But let's not totally deceive ourselves. Of course the positive balance is great but FNMA has tons of liabilities. So we must consider that when analyzing the stock. But the major downfall that is holding down its stock price is the negative 467 billion dollar debt cloud they have surrounding them. Sure, they have assets in the trillions of dollars, but that doesn't matter when your liabilities are also in the trillions of dollars *and* your debt is in the hundreds of billions of dollars.

Now that we know how to look at a balance sheet and cash flow statement and pick out information, we can go to the next level. First, we need to analyze the three years that are shown on the financing website. Are their net assets increasing? Are their net liabilities decreasing? Is the debt decreasing? These are the main key points to look at, especially when valuing a penny stock company. Sure, they may not be bringing in billions of dollars in income and yeah, they may not have billions of dollars in shareholder equity, and sure, they may have a ton of debt.

But are they taking steps to increase their income and pay down their debt? Their financials will show that by revealing an increase in total assets each year and a decrease in total liabilities each year. That is all you can really ask for in a penny stock that is trading as the cheap levels that this book is profiling. Remember, however, that the company's reporting numbers are current and that the company itself is current. If not, these numbers can be deceiving.

So, once we do that and we have the three years. We then try to calculate a book value. The book value is the net worth of a company (total assets minus total liabilities) divided by the number of shares outstanding. Often, with penny stocks, this will end up being a negative number.

Without boring you with the calculations and the mathematics as you can calculate it yourself using the formula in the above paragraph, Disney has a current book value of $26.44 as of 2014 and an old book value of $23.38 in 2012. Now, if you type in "Buffett's Books intrinsic value calculator" into a search engine, you will be brought to a website. The top section needs the two book values and the time between them to calculate the average book value change. Once you have that information, you then have to look up the 10 year federal note yield (which can change daily and can be found using a google search). Once you have the note yield, you can then use the bottom calculator to determine the intrinsic value of a company. In this case, Disney comes out to $32.24 a share.

Of course there are other aspects other than finances that determine the price of a company's stock. But based solely on intrinsic value, Disney with a price per share of over $100 is vastly overvalued.

This calculation becomes tricky when we are dealing with negative numbers. For example, NSAV has a net value of negative $551,000. It has a total number of shares outstanding of $1.06 billion, which can be found in the "key statistics" tab on yahoo finance on the company's page or in the "Company Profile" table on OTC Markets on the company's page. The current book value comes to -$0.0005. It has an old book value of $0.000124. Therefore, it is becoming less valuable over time and the calculation on Buffett's website does not like to deal with negatives.

Therefore, it is recommended to only use Buffett's Books with companies that are increasing in net assets and are decreasing their net liabilities, have a positive cash flow with no negative numbers in any of its income, and have a value over a dollar. For pure penny stocks that are trading under a dollar a share, simply make sure that the balance between the net assets and the net liabilities is becoming more positive over time and do not worry about Buffett's intrinsic calculator.

Play with these calculations and looking up financials in your preferred financial website. Get as proficient with these numbers as you can. The process seems daunting and the first time a trader does it, it will take forever. But over time, a trader can get this process down to less than five minutes a stock. Perfect practice makes perfect.

Share Structure

When analyzing the share structure, you can use many websites. The two most convenient, that I have found, are yahoo finance and OTC markets. In yahoo finance, you would look in the key statistics tab on the left after searching for the particular ticker of your interest.

However, for this explanation, we are going to use OTC markets. Visit OTCMARKETS.com and type in your ticker of preference. Then on the left hand column, click company profile. In the company profile, you will find the company's reporting status which tells you if they are current, their latest share structure report, their market value, their outstanding shares as "shares outstanding", their float, their authorized shares, the number of shareholders, and many more statistics.

Authorized shares is the total number of shares that a company is allowed to issue and is agreed upon when they issue their charter. This number can change, however, it is more difficult to do than simply issuing shares.

Outstanding shares is the total number of shares owned by all of its shareholders. Or, in effect, the number of shares that have already been issued from their authorized shares.

The Float is the number of shares that are traded by retail. Retail, to put it simply, is the trader that does not have esoteric information about the company. In other words, the float is controlled by non-insiders such as those other than the CEO, employees of the company and their respective families, and debtors. In effect, retail is you and me.

Often, on OTCMARKETS.com, if a company is not current or has failed to update the SEC, their main page will show a stop signing warning traders that they are not current and may be withholding information from investors.

As of February 2015, traders can see this stop sign if you look up the stock ticker symbol LUSI. However, PVSP is also not current but does not have a stop sign. You can tell that PVSP is not current because their last shares outstanding report date was in 2013, which you can see next to their number of shares outstanding.

We will first analyze Disney (DIS). For some reason, OTC markets does not show Disney's share structure. So we will look it up on Yahoo Finance. On Yahoo Finance's website on the DIS ticker page under key statistics, it shows 1.7 billion shares outstanding, 1.57 billion share float, but it does not show the authorized shares.

PVSP has a share structure as such:

>   Authorized shares: 800,000,000

>   Shares outstanding: 799,499,997

>   Float: 403,528,069

IJJP has a share structure as such:

>   Authorized shares: 3,000,000,000

>   Shares outstanding: 2,187,251,895

>   Float: 1,799,307,525

VMGI has a share structure as such:

>   Authorized shares: 4,000,000,000

>   Shares outstanding: 1,729,821,337

>   Float: 1,518,560,674

TNKE has a share structure as such:

>   Authorized shares: 995,000,000

>   Shares outstanding: 396,736,402

>   Float: 5,490,400

All shares are as of February 16, 2015. Remember though, PVSP has not issued an update of their share structure since 2013, which is 2 years ago. That's huge. They could have increased their authorized shares into the billions and, subsequently, increased the float substantially. Why would a company do this? They would do this for two reasons; one to increase their cash flow into the company, and two, to pay off debt.

All of the above companies, with the exception of Disney, are trading under a penny. TNKE's current close on February 16, 2015 is $0.0009 a share, IJJP's close is $0.0031 a share, VMGI's close is $0.0007 a share, and PVSP's close is $0.0002 a share. The very low share price could mean many things. There could be considerable amount of debt, which was described earlier as okay as long as the debt is being reduced over time. There could be no or little revenue. Trading or investing in companies with absolutely no revenue is too much speculation and risk for an intelligent trader to partaken in. However, little revenue is okay as long as it is increasing, on average, over time. What do I mean by on average? If you analyze five years of revenue for a company, the numbers could look like the following:

> 2010 Revenue: $10,000
>
> 2011 Revenue: $4,000
>
> 2012 Revenue: $11,000
>
> 2013 Revenue: $9,000
>
> 2014 Revenue: $21,000

Then you add up all of the yearly revenues and divide by the number of years. The average revenue in this case is $11,000. $11,000 is more than the first year in question. So, in all, the revenues, although they increase and decrease yearly, are increasing over time. In the penny stock land where a lot of companies do not even have revenue plans in place, the fact that a particular company is actually bringing in revenue is amazing. However, we cannot be subdued by this lucrative perception. The revenues must be increasing, on average, over time. This proves that they are a growth company. Why would any trader trade a company that is not bringing in increasing revenues unless, of course, it is to ride a quick pump. The pump is ideal for the daily trader but is subpar for the worker trader who cannot sit in front of a screen all day and trade.

Likewise, we also analyze the debt. And we should analyze the debt for the same number of years that we analyze the revenue. As we mentioned before, negative number will be written in parenthesis instead of with a negative sign in front. So a five year debt analysis would look like this:

2010 debt: (210,119, 199)

2011 debt: (187,841,220)

2012 debt: (189,222,569)

2013 debt: (150,000,888)

2014 debt: (151,311,005)

At first glance, we can see that the debt has been reduced from 210 million dollars down to 151 million dollars, or 59 million dollars reduction of debt. Additionally, if we add up all of the debt and divide by the number of years, we get an average yearly debt of $177,698.976.20. That average is less than the initial year's debt.

So in all, with the above simulated scenario, we like the fact that the revenue is increasing and the debt is decreasing; even though the average revenue is only

$11,000 and the average debt is a whopping $177,768,976. Welcome to penny stock land. There is a reason why this hypothetical stock is probably trading at under $0.001 a share.

That being said, if we look at the balance sheet, it will automatically tell us the difference in net assets (revenue plus other assets) minus the liabilities (debt minus other liabilities). We can use this number to analyze the penny stock rather than calculate the difference between the revenue and debt because this figure calculates this for us.

Now, for the above share structures, the best one of the bunch is TNKE. As I mention in "Penny Stock Players", we want a low float. The lower the float, the more volatility the stock will have which means the better chance you have of making money quickly. No one wants to be stuck in a penny stock with little to no movement for months to years.

From the above listed tickers, TNKE provides the lowest float of them all with a float of only 5,490,400 shares. Let me tell you that this is a ridiculously low float for a penny stock, especially one trading at $0.0009 a share. I hope it is accurate.

***NOTE: Even though companies can be current, their current financial statement and share structure is only required to be reported quarterly at the earliest. Therefore, if it has been two months since the numbers have been updated, it is likely that they have changed and not in the traders' favor. A call to the transfer agent may afford you an update but this is not always accurate as there is not law require them to be truthful.

Now that we know that TNKE has a low float, we then can analyze its cash flow. Using the net tangible asset method that is already calculated for us on the balance sheet that is posted on, for this stock, OTC markets, we see the follow net assets (represented as thousands of dollars):

2011 Net Assets: (41)

2012 Net Assets: (113)

2013 Net Assets: 1,509

2014 Net Assets: 1,452

That's right! TNKE has now moved from a negative balance in 2011 and 2012 to a positive balance in 2013 and 2014. If we average out the net assets and divide by the number of years [4], we get ($37,759.75) or -$37,759.75. This number is more positive than the original ($41,000) that the company started with. Therefore, the net balance is becoming more positive over time. Because we used the net asset balance, we do not know if the revenues are increasing, the debt is decreasing, or both. But in this case, it does not matter. All that matters is that the balance sheet is getting more positive over time because either the average debt is less than the earliest year we analyzed and/or that the average income or revenue has increased from that same year.

TNKE satisfies all three of the above categories. It has a low float, relatively speaking. Its debt is decreasing. Its income is increasing. And its balance sheet is becoming more positive.

So, for now, TNKE is on our radar. We can automatically dismiss PVSP because it is not current and so, we do not know how many shares are actually out there. But if they become current and they report favorable numbers, our thoughts on PVSP may change. We can dismiss IJJP because it has already risen 500% and, although it can provide a good trade from its current levels due to the momentum it has built, it is not going to be the discussion of "The Art of Bottom Feeding" with the exception of analyzing the chart and looking at its financials and share structure.

Therefore, the final company we have left is VMGI. For the purposes of being brief, we will quickly analyze VMGI's net tangible assets, which are posted on OTC markets.

VMGI's net tangible assets are thus (in thousands of dollars):

> 2011 Net Tangible Assets: (1,134)
>
> 2102 Net Tangible Assets: (1,244)
>
> 2013 Net Tangible Assets: (1,290)
>
> 2014 Net Tangible Assets: (1,438)

On first glance, we can see that the numbers are becoming more negative over time. Therefore, we do not even need to calculate the difference to see that the average is going to be more negative than the initial year. But we will calculate it anyway. The average net tangible assets is ($1,276.50). Yes it is decreasing over time, but not to a ridiculous extent. The debt is in the millions, yes, but we should not make the full mistake of completely dismissing this stock right away. We've already talked about the true pump. Therefore, before we dismiss this stock, let's look at the charts of both TNKE and VMGI.

We have already looked at VMGI's chart but I will post it again. The following is VMGI's weekly chart and TNKE's daily chart in succession and in that order:

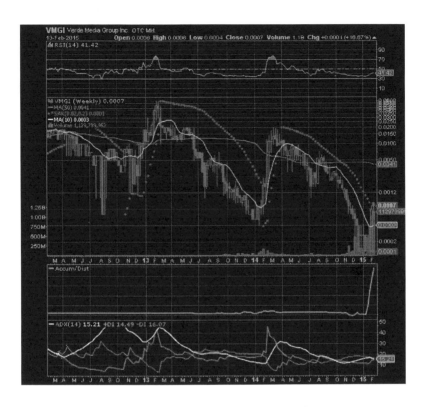

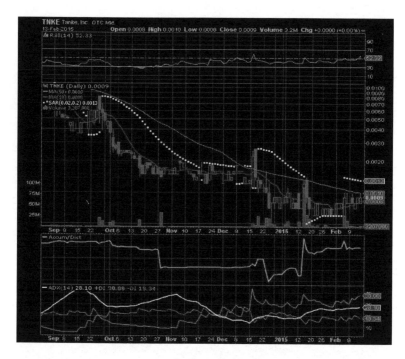

Here's quick question to test your skills on chart reading. Answer this question before reading further: Do either of these charts provide a potential trade and, if so, which one provides the greatest short term potential?

We have already analyzed VMGI's chart. But we will take a quick look at it again because repetition is the mother of skill. The parabolic SAR is positive, the 10 day MA is curling up towards the 50 day MA for a potential cross, the volume is insanely high, the RSI is low, the AD is high, the ADX line is curling down, the DI lines are crossing in a positive fashion, and the price has bounced off of the complete floor bottom.

TNKE provides a slightly similar chart. The parabolic SAR is negative, the 10 day MA is only a few days away from crossing up through the 50 day MA, the volume is low, the RSI is neither low nor high, the AD line is high, the ADX

DI lines are moving away from each other, and the price is trading sideways in a slight uptrend.

Initially, because the TNKE chart is posted in the daily timeframe, one would think that it has the most potential short term. However, that is not so. TNKE's weekly chart has only 1 positive sign, the parabolic SAR. But the daily chart has a 4 to 3 positive to negative ratio whereas the VMGI weekly chart has a 5 to 2 positive to negative ratio. This can change drastically if TNKE's volume begins to rapidly increase.

***NOTE: The author has knowingly and purposefully left out the daily chart for VMGI and the weekly chart for TNKE for the weekly TNKE chart is very choppy at best and does not provide a good trade based on charting. However, the daily VMGI tells another story and provides a very good trade. But for the case of bottom feeding where we buy and hold for longer periods, we prefer the weekly chart over the daily chart if it provides a positive trade position.

Therefore, the VMGI chart, although slightly more negative financially and key statistically, provides a much better trade opportunity based on the chart in the short term. Momentum will be discussed further in this book. However, let this first practical momentum lesson be learned: *always* trade momentum over financials. The financials and share structure information is presented so that you can inform yourself of your trades and do your own due diligence. Ideally, all stars will be aligned. But the probability of finding such a stock with all stars aligned is like the probability of finding another earth-like planet in another galaxy. But, like these earth-like planets, although rare, they are out there and can be found.

Additionally, long term trades develop over time. Yes, because VMGI's chart is of the weekly timeframe, it looks as though it could become positive and develop into a true pump over time. However, only time, itself, will determine this to be true.

Penny stock trading takes as much faith as it does skill and knowledge. A trader can have the perfect set up with the chart, have the perfect financials with the company, have momentum on his or her side, but immediately after purchasing shares in this company, that company can release terrible news and completely destroy the setup. Nothing in penny stock land is always as it seems. So faith and emotional control is crucial.

More on the share structure: Often, if a company has a lot of outstanding shares and a lot of shares in the float, they also have a lot of debt. By selling shares, the company helps themselves to pay off their debt. This debt is converted into shares and sold to the market and is often termed "Asher" or "Toxic Debt" in the esoteric penny stocks trader language.

A very important key to finding the bottom of a chart is to wait for news or a press release that states that the company has finished with their convertibles. What this means is that no more debt is to be converted into shares to be sold onto the market unless more debt is taken out. But in this case, if more debt financing is received, then the company must disclose this to their shareholders in news or a press release.

But once a company has finished paying off Asher and is no longer converting their shares, you can be rest assured that the ticker price has bottomed and will most likely turn north. If the share structure is terrible, meaning a lot of shares in the float or shares outstanding, it may take longer for the price to move from the bottom. But if you trade a stock with a terrible share structure, I'd have to ask why and wonder if you were awake when you were reading this book. You always trade a low float, always, always, always.

So, once a stock ticker has found a bottom and has converted all of its debt, there's one more thing to watch out for; this is the reverse split. Make sure that the company is not going to do a reverse split. You can do your due diligence in full. This includes looking through the filings, news, and press releases, researching the CEO, and even calling the CEO to get as much information out of him or her as he or she can disclose over the phone.

Then you must wait for volume to pour into the ticker. If you don't wait for volume, you risk waiting up to forever for it to move. We all want the complete full breadth of profits. But if you try to catch the absolutely complete dead bottom, you risk a lot. So a wise trader waits for confirmation that the stock is about to bounce. This is done by waiting for the volume to hit the chart and for the PSAR to flip to the bottom.

***NOTE: If a company announces that they are going to perform a reverse split, regardless of how much you are down, it is wise to sell your shares. You can always buy back in later once the reverse split is completed. However, this too is risky because the share price can be watered down again until your position becomes worthless. But as witnessed in 2015, a stock price can provide explosive gains after a reverse split. It is still wise for a trader to wait for the dust to settle after the completion of a reverse split to see if the price drops precipitously.

Minimize risk: Do not buy into a reverse split. Buy into low floats with low Outstanding and Authorized shares. Make sure the company is current and they are bringing in some kind of revenue.

Chapter 7 – News & The CEO

News releases are one of the most powerful catalysts. Usually a news release is preceded by huge volume that you can see on the chart. When you look up a chart and you see massive volume but no reason for it, then you can rest assured that news is coming. This news is often in the form of news or a press release, but sometimes it can be hinted at through Twitter or a blog post.

News and press releases can often be seen on Ihub.com, or any of the financial websites such as Yahoo finance, MSN money, market wire, or OTC markets. They can also be seen often on your trading website such as E*TRADE or Scott trade, etc.

When you look up a chart and you see huge volume pouring into the ticker and this tips you off that news is coming, be careful that the price per share has not risen dramatically before buying in or you risk losing money in the short term. This is because front loaders, who know that the news is coming, will buy only to sell at a certain percentage once new buyers who recently became aware of the news or press release buys in and increases the share price still further.

The insider selling, however, is usually powerful enough to drop the price back to its original pre-news position.

***NOTE: The author's reference to insiders does not necessarily mean the illegal trading based on esoteric knowledge. It also encompasses traders who buy the rumor and sell the news; a common saying in penny land.

So how powerful can these news releases be? Let's take a look at a few companies, their news releases, and their corresponding charts.

We will first analyze the company with the stock ticker symbol IJJP.

On January 20, 2012, IJJP released a news piece with the headline that stated they were ceasing the issuance of 504 stock. Then we didn't hear from them again until November of 2014. That's more than two whole years without hearing a single peep from the company.

In November, IJJP released two news releases, one stating that they developed a new B2B Network as a subscription based service, and the other also talked about their B2B Network. And as you can see from the following chart that the volume picked up and price reacted as well.

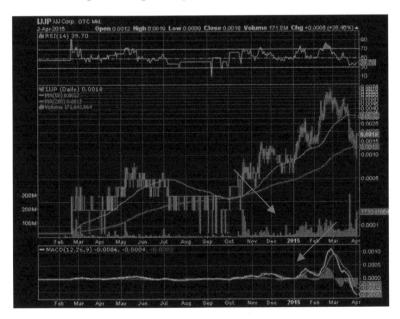

Coincidently, the news dropped shorty after a death cross (the 50 day moving average crossing down through the

200 day moving average). However, due to the positive reaction to the news, the ticker responded beautifully and the chart reversed into a golden cross (the 50 day moving average crossing up through the 200 day moving average).

Then IJJP released a series of news releases detailing their medial cannabis deals and revenue streams in late 2014 and early 2015. As you can see from the above chart, the price continued to climb in traditional pump fashion. A sharp increase in price as reaction to the news followed by a slight pull back (we call this consolidation), and then another sharp increase, rinse and repeat.

On February 25, 2015, IJJP announced that they were retiring nearly 400 million shares. This means that the shares that are retired will no longer be available to be traded. This lowers the shares outstanding and the float and, subsequently, increases the share price.

IJJP continued to release news about new partners in 2015. They also announced the retiring of 500 million more shares. These are all excellent news releases.

However, IJJP also started releasing news and press releases detailing information about the way the stock is being traded. On both March 10 and March 20 of the year 2015, they announced press releases that mentioned they are trying to rid the trading of their company of short sellers and that the price has closed above the squeeze trigger price.

In my opinion, the last two press releases were stupid and unfortunate. Why would, or should, a company be so interested in the way their shares are being traded unless all they care about is investor sentiment and stock price value? On the surface, this seems smart. But if we think deeper about the situation, we, as traders, will feel like the company is manipulating us. Rather than focusing on building their business and generating revenue streams, they are more focused on how their stock is being traded. This was the mistake they made.

Let's look at the IJJP chart as of April 12, 2015:

The white circles correspond with the last two new release dates and the white box shows the *huge* sell of date. As you can see, these news releases were not taken too kindly and the price has plummeted from around a half a penny per share to $0.0012 a share. This is a price drop of -76%!

The news can be as devastatingly bearish triggering as it can be bullish triggering. The trick is to see the trader sentiment change and to get out before the huge selloff. It must be stated that it is potentially possible that the news releases were coincidental and that the pump just ran out of steam. But given that this happens a lot, a causation relationship is more likely than a correlation one.

A very important question is, how do traders get out in time?

The answer lies within the chart. You see the small pump that started around March 9th? Well, follow that pump until you see the *very* small green volume day. The price had been climbing for four days. But the small volume suggests that, although the day was still green, traders were losing interested in the stock. A vigilant trader would have seen that and sold on that day or on the next day.

Since the marijuana industry is hot again in early 2015, let's take a look at another marijuana company. This company is called Totally Hemp Crazy, Inc. and trades under the ticker symbol THCZ.

Let's first look at the chart for THCZ:

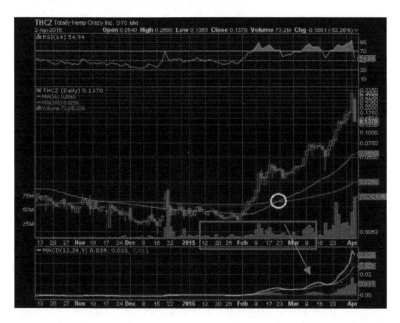

Now for the news. On January 27, 2015, THCZ dropped this headline: "Totally Hemp Crazy Inc. (THCZ) Signs Agreement With Mr. Checkout for Distribution of Rocky Mountain High Beverage Drinks". Coincidently, late January started the pump.

Then every news release in February and March of 2015 mentioned their Rocky Mountain High beverage and combined it with the likes of Willie Nelson and Amazon.com.

Anyone who knows anything about penny stocks knows that when a penny stock company strikes a deal with a celebrity or a big company, that penny stock company's price per share, more often than not, skyrockets. And as you can see by THCZ's chart, this company was no different.

But, just like with IJJP, THCZ released a news releases pertaining to the way the stock is trading and look at that huge selloff in very early April. The news release headlined that they were not engaged in any stock promotions.

Again, this was stupid. I have to ask why they are so concerned with sentiment of their investors other than because of the workings and revenues of the company. Anything that pertains to the actual way the stock is trading is bad news and suggests that the company cares too much about its stock price. Of course traders want the company to care about the stock price and we want the price to rise. But we want the company to increase the price through deals and revenue, **not** through the manipulation of trading.

Here is the updated THCZ chart as of April 12, 2015:

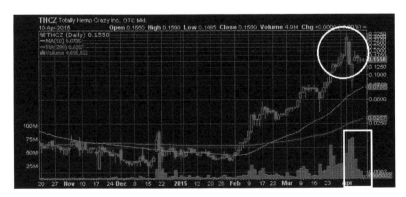

The price has held steadily after the two major dump selloff days. But look at that volume. It has practically dropped off the map and doesn't even exist. Only time will tell if it picks back up. It's a little different because it is occurring at a consolidation period. So this could mean that the sellers are done selling and that the bulls are ready to push the price up some more. But I would wait for confirmation of this by increased volume and any of the previously mentioned bullish candle sticks. The bullish engulfing is my favorite.

Because this is so much fun for me, I will detail one more company. And from these three companies, you can learn what to extrapolate from the news and what to look for in a headline that sways public opinion in a positive way.

Let's first look at the chart. Here is the stock chart for the penny stock company Creative Edge Nutrition with the stock ticker symbol FITX:

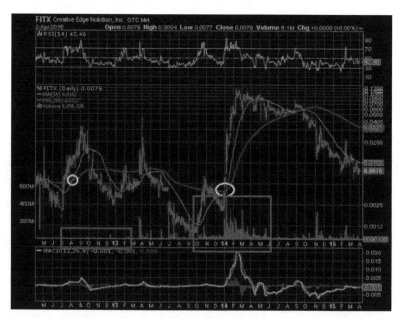

Now for the news. On January 29, 2014, FITX released this headline: "GrowLife and CEN Biotech Announce Collaboration on the World's Largest and Most Advanced Legal Cannabis Production Facility". A few days later and for nearly two months, FITX's price shot straight up with **no** consolidation!

That's pretty much all the investors and traders needed to know. No more news was released until March. But look at that price action, wow!! The price ran from $0.002-ish to around 12 cents a share.

Then traders began to take profits and the news became less positive. They announced that they were having zoning issues with their facility and that Canada had denied them a licensed under their MMPR program. This, they initially tried to fight but then they released another press release stating they had retracted their judicial review request to try to overrule the denial.

Looks like traders and investors did not take too kindly to this and the price has continued to drop.

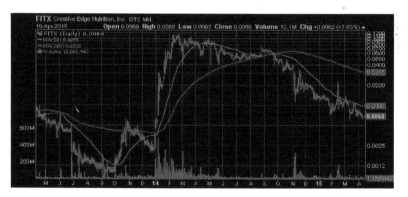

As of April 12, 2015, FITX's price has fallen from 12 cents to $0.0068 a share. This is a drop of 94% from their high price of 12 cents in February of 2014.

So as you can see the price of a security can dramatically be effected by news and press releases either positively or negatively depending on trader and investor sentiment. If we perceive the news is good, we tend to buy and hold for great gains. If we perceive the news to be bad, we either don't buy or we sell the shares we have.

The reason that most stocks don't just drop to nothing when bad news or unfavorable news hits is because there's always a second wave of traders who, upon seeing a drop in the share price, buy back in and try to push the price back up for what is commonly called round two. But once these traders take their profits or losses, the price begins to crumble faster. Then sometimes a ticker will have a round three, a round four, etc...You can see these rounds on FITX's chart.

In November of 2014, there was a huge increase in share volume and the price had a bit of a jump. But it also failed. Then in February of 2015, again traders tried to push the price up but profit takers pushed it back down again.

Minimize risk: Conventional wisdom dictates that traders buy the rumor and sell the news. So, wait until there is a dip in price after news is released before buying, or buy into a rumor.

The CEO can be found by looking in OTC Markets or Yahoo on the page of ticker in question. Then, once the CEO is found, a simple Google search can reveal a great deal of information. Look for CEOs with a long history of driving companies to success. His or her track record will speak for itself.

Try to avoid stocks with CEOs who are shady and have proven time and time again to not have the ability to build a successful company. A failure or two in the beginning is fine. No one knows how to build a successful company from scratch the first time. It's only those who surround themselves with great people who are successful the first time.

But again, be cautious with CEOs and make sure that both sides, the good and the bad, are taken into account. A CEO can not only not be a good business person, but they can also have a history of selling their stock, diluting their stock, taking out too much debt for investors and revenue to cover the costs, and many more business sins that destroy investor value.

But also do not believe everything that is said on every websites about a CEO. The credibility of the website should also be noted.

Researching a CEO is as simple as a Google search.

Chapter 8 – Momentum: Trade with the Crowd

Trading with momentum is the key to explosive gains. The thing about bottom feeding though is that we get in before the momentum hits. But you don't want to get in too soon or you will be forced to hold bags, hopes, and dreams that the volume will flow into the chart soon.

So how do we avoid becoming a bag holder?

We wait for confirmation of the reversal *before* buying in. Yes, you may lose a few percentages on your gains. However, losing say two to ten percent on a reversal of a bottomed chart is way more desirable than holding a position for six months with no movement because no one cares about the ticker you put your money into.

To play it safe, *always* wait for confirmation. The trick is to keep multiple bottomed out stocks on your watch list and keep an eye on them for a reversal pattern. This can come in the form of a lower moving average cross up through a higher moving average such as the 10 day moving average cross up through the 50 day moving average or the golden cross.

Or you can wait for increased volume and any of the reversal pattern candle sticks to hit such as bullish engulfing (yes, it's still my favorite), the hammer or reverse hammer (at the bottom of a downtrend or consolidation only!), a shooting star, and the doji. Any of these indicators can signal a reversal off of a downtrend if the chart is bottomed and there is sudden increased volume.

Remember, **do not** use these candle sticks as a bullish indicators if they occur in an uptrend. Only use them as downtrend reversals into an uptrend.

For the best confirmation of these candles, wait for two or three to hit in a row with increasing or steady volume that is higher than what was pouring into the chart during the downtrend. For example, if you see a reverse red hammer during a downtrend with slightly increased volume, then a shooting star with the same volume, then bullish engulfing with the same or increased volume, then you have as much confirmation as can be reasonably expected for a buy in on a reversal pattern.

What would make this even better is if the 10 day moving average is curling up and the 50 day moving average is either still moving down or leveling out; or if the 50 day moving average is getting ready to cross up through the 200 day moving average and the volume is increasing.

Remember though, the crosses are lagging indicators. This means, more often than not, the increase in price per share will not occur on the same day as the cross. It will occur a few days or weeks after, depending on the timeframe you are looking at on the chart (either the daily chart or weekly chart).

Momentum is suggested by the increased volume and is confirmed by two things. One, an increase in price per share. And two, the amount of chatter and buzz surrounding the ticker on social websites such as Ihub.com, Twitter.com, and Facebook.com.

And the final piece of the puzzle is great news released by the company. If you are following a downtrend on a ticker and see any of the bullish reversal candles followed by another confirmation candle, steadily or majorly increasing volume, buzz surrounding the ticker on social websites, and then great news hits the wires, you can be rest assured that the chart is going to reverse and the prices are going to correct to the upside.

These factors are what create the momentum. And once the momentum starts, it doesn't slow down for quite a while as we saw in the previous chapter's chart examples. Those tickers didn't just have great news that triggered the uptrends, they also had plenty of buzz on social media websites, a great looking chart with multiple bullish indicators, and plenty of volume.

So why leave this to chance?

Find the charts that are on a downtrend and are nearly sold all the way down to the bottom. Then, find traders on social media websites that have tons of followers and also like to play these bottomed charts. Then once they alert a bottomed ticker to their subscribers, make sure it is on your watch list.

I'm not saying you should trust these traders with every ticker they alert. Far from it. What I am saying though, is if they alert a ticker and that ticker passes your buy in tests and has bottomed out, it not only saves you time because you do not have to go looking for the ticker, but it also helps keep you from holding bags.

A bag holder is someone who just holds their position for up to years because there is no trader interest and, therefore, there is no price action. However, if a trader has tons of followers and alerts a stock, his followers, more likely than not, will buy into that ticker.

And as their followers buy into the ticker the price will increase. Therefore, if the ticker is already on your watch list, and is alerted by a trader with tons of followers, you are already ready to purchase it before his followers get in.

Again, I reiterate, make sure the trader is trustworthy by watching a few of his alerts before buying in any of them to make sure that they actually do reverse. Also, make sure that when he or she alerts the ticker that the price actually does respond positively and that his followers do buy into the stock, which you can see as an increase in volume.

Once you've verified the trader's credentials, you can then trade one of his alerts. But make sure the alert passes **your** tests for your trading style. Do not start buying tickers just because a trader has proven herself to be a great stock picker. It only takes one mistake, one buy in without checking the stock to make sure it's right for you, for you to lose on the trade. And the worst feeling in the world is to feel like someone else is responsible for your loss on a trade.

No one is responsible for your trading except for you. Therefore, the following of a trader's alert serves only to save you time and to ensure that volume hits the ticker. That is all! You cannot remain profitable by blindly following another trader. Their opinions should be taken as such and should be fact checked by you and by your trading system.

If you are comfortable taking the risk of holding a ticker before volume hits without too much fear that the volume will never hit, then so be it. That's your trading style, so buy in before the volume. But remember, you may be holding that ticker indefinitely. And make sure you do your full due diligence so that you know for a fact that no reverse split is coming.

But for most traders and trading situations, we should trade with the momentum. But do not buy in at the top. Just because a ticker has increased in price doesn't mean it will continue to do so. And just because volume is high, does not mean that the volume will continue to be high.

There are some tickers out there that can be front loaded by traders. You will suddenly see a huge volume spike day for no reason. This is your warning. **Do not** buy into this type of increased volume on a ticker thinking that you are getting in before others know about it, especially if price has also increased. This is probably just some front loaders who are ready to hit the sell button as you as you purchase your shares, or have already set their sell so that you will be buying their shares. In this case, *always* wait for confirmation through social media buzz (more than a handful of traders), continued increase in volume, and multiple reversal candles, and all of the other indicators that have been outlined in this book.

Momentum can stifle any attempt to crash a stock, but only for a limited amount of time. Traders love to buy dips and support a stock on the bid at a previous support level. So if you have bought a bottomed chart and have ridden momentum up a ways, but you have not hit your percentage gain as dictated by your system, look at level 2 and see how much bid support you have at the indicated support price that is showing on the chart.

Here is IJJP's chart showing support and resistance levels:

***NOTE: The paperback version is black and white. The bottom line is support, the top line is resistance and every line in between is both support and resistance. For clarity purposes, if the line touches the skinny part of the candle (a price that was reached but did not sustain through the close) at the bottom of the candle, it is support. And if the same happens at the top of the candle, it is resistance.

The orange lines are resistance lines and the yellow lines are support lines. These lines were drawn where the price hit and bounce up or down from. However, if you draw the lines where the candles either opened or closed, you will see that the lines line up perfectly in most cases, as is the case at the line that is second to the top.

This is what happens: When there is a resistant point (price), and that point is broken to the upside, then that resistance point becomes a support point. Additionally, when there is a support point, and that point is broken to the downside, then that support point becomes a resistance point.

So, if we were trading IJJP, and let's say we saw the bullish engulfing around November 10 of 2014 and we bought in. Then we decided to sell half of our shares at resistance and buy back in with the profits at support. We would have been afforded four buy in opportunities. And five selling opportunities.

Here's how it would work: each support level held, and once we saw that the price bounced up from the support level (the previous resistance level that we sold at), we would buy back in. However, on the second to final sell around February 20 something, we saw that the price continued to dip but never touched the support below it. However, once it did touch it on around March 24 or 25 of 2015, it *never* bounce up from it. This this is a clear sign of a weakening trend and we should have sold for our fifth sell and complete exit from this position. Without even looking at any other indicators that may have been bearish such as an overbought OBV line or RSI line, we would know to sell because it broke support and never recovered.

However, IJJP would have still afforded us great profits.

Another way to trade this IJJP trend, would have been to buy in, then to sell at a predetermined percentage gain. But we would only sell enough of our shares to get our original position out, then we would ride free shares all the way up until is broke our support level at the top.

We do this like this: We buy IJJP at $0.0007 let's say because of the bullish engulfing for $1,000. Then we hold until $0.0014, which was the first clear resistance point that afforded us a nice profit. But we only sell half of our position. Why? Because since the price has doubled, half of our position will give us our thousand dollars back.

Now we have free shares that we never paid for, except, of course, for our trade fees. Then we hold that amount of shares all the way up until the support at the top fails. And we sell at $0.003. Or, if you would like to be knit picky about it, there are two other slight support level that formed above the $0.003 level. These are at the $0.0035 and $0.005 levels, respectively.

So if we traded this perfectly, we would have bought at .0007, sold half of our shares at $0.0014, and sold the rest at $0.005.

With $1,000, we would have purchased 1,428,571 shares. Then we set our sell of 714,285 shares for #0.0014 a share. Then we would hold the remaining 714,286 shares until the $0.005 resistance hit for the second time. So the first sell gave us back our thousand dollars. And the second sell gave us a gross profit of $3,571.43.

Congratulations, you just made over three times your money by following momentum and a system of trading that afforded you the most profits in the relatively safest way. But timing these buys and sells perfectly is tricky and is easier said than none. Be careful.

Another system, which I now prefer, is almost exactly like the one described above. Except in this system, we not only sell half of our shares so that we can get our original position back, but we also sell a little bit more so that we can take some profits off as well. So what we would do is sell up to 75% of our shares and then ride the rest as free shares for as long as with like.

That way, since they are free shares, if the stock crashes on us and we lose all of our profits, we've already sold our original position and got some profits out of the stock. And so if and when it crashes, we do not lose any money.

This method simultaneously gets you out of your position and gives you profits. Then you can take that original position plus your profits and trade another stock. Or you can take your original position and trade another stock, and take profits and pocket them. This is the most powerful way of trading because it allows you to not only make profits on paper but it also allows you to pocket your profits. And by pocketing your profits, once you get good and start trading with a lot of money, the profits you make on each trade can pay for your living expenses, or you can keep them in your account and build up your portfolio.

So if you are just now starting out and you don't have a lot of cash, by trading this method, you can slowly build up your capital so that you are making trades with decent amounts of money. And as you win with each trade, you can take a profit out of it and put it in your pocket to pay for your living expenses. This is a great way of supplementing your income if you work a job or replacing your income and quitting your job. But you must first become good at trading and know that you're going to be profitable.

How to know that you're being profitable? The best test is if you hit on nine out of 10 trades. If you can hit on nine out ten trades then you are now profitable and if your capital is built up enough, you can now trade for a living.

At this point, once you get good enough, you no longer have to hit nine out 10 trades. Your capital will be built up enough so that you can probably only have to hit 60% of your trades in order to do it for a living. And by trading this method, you are afforded another benefit.

But before we describe that benefit let me explain to you one more thing. That thing will come in the next chapter as we discussed "Penny Stock Players" rules and a system of trading that allows you to win half as many times as you lose and still remain either profitable or even.

Minimize risk: Have a rule of a percentage increase that you will not buy into if the price hits that percentage increase or higher. Buy at support and sell at resistance. Do not buy a stock that is overbought as dictated by the previously discussed indicators.

Chapter 9 – Penny Stock Players Rules Explained:

In this chapter, I will explain the 20 rules that were listed in my first book entitled "Penny Stock Players". These rules will first be listed in a numbered format. Then I will describe them one by one in full detail. And finally, at the end of the chapter, I will reveal a trading trick that will allow you to either make profits or break even on your trades even if you lose more often than you win.

Here are the 20 rules that I will be explaining in full detail:

1. History repeats itself (pattern trading)

2. People drive buying and selling (emotion)

3. Buy at Support and Sell at Resistance (these can be seen on the chart)

4. Short rallies not sell offs

5. Do not buy into a major moving average or sell into one

6. Do not chase momentum

7. Exhaustion gaps get filled

8. Trends test the point of last resistance and/or support

9. Trade with the tick, not against it

10. If the trader has to look, it isn't there

11. Sell the second high, buy the second low

12. The trend is the trader's friend in the last hour (power hour)

13. Avoid the open [The open is when the stock exchange opens in the AM]

14. Downtrends reverse after a top, two lower highs, and a double bottom (chart)

15. Buyers (Bulls) live above the 200 MA Sellers (Bears) live below it (moving average)

16. Price has a memory

17. Big volume kills moves by causing the ticker to trade sideways (equal buying and selling)

18. Trends never turn on a dime

19. Bottoms take longer to form than tops

20. Beat the crowd into and out of the door

ONE: History repeats itself

Not only does this apply to the history of humans, as in the case of economic collapses like those of any fiat currency systems, it also applies to stock prices. For an analogy far away from the financial system as possible, I present you this: In American football, especially the National Football League (NFL), scouts – those professionals who are employed to study professional or collegial football players – often tout a truth that if they see it once, they will likely see it again. Therefore, if they see a player make amazing plays, they feel that they will see it again. Likewise, if they see the player shirk, they also feel they will see *that* again.

To bring us back to stock trading, we traders feel that if we see a stock hit a certain price, then we will see it again.

Therefore, the chart plays a very important and practical role in stock trading.

Not only do we use the chart for all the above scenarios, we also use it to see support and resistance levels and where the chart *can* head, not just where it is or where it will head.

This is so very important because in penny land, especially sub-penny land, as the pattern is everything. A stock price pattern tells the whole story. What is the price doing? That's key! Is it in a downtrend, well, how far down has it hit before? If it breaks down below that point, watch out! Also, how far up has it hit? And if it's currently in an uptrend and it breaks that previous all-time high, we call this a blue sky breakout because there are no more resistance points.

Here is an example of a blue sky breakout. The orange line represents the previous high (the point that I was talking about that if you see it once, you will see it again). This is the two year chart for IJJP:

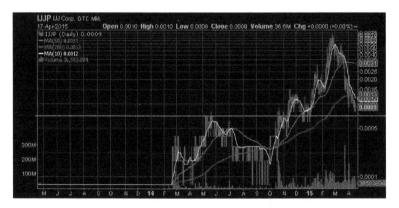

As you can see, the company didn't trade for at least half the 2013 trading year. Then volume poured into the chart in early 2014. In May of 2014, IJJP hit an average high of around $0.00065, which is where the orange line lies.

Then IJJP dipped to about $0.0002. However, it quickly rebounded in the wake of a 10 day moving average cross up through the 200 day and 50 day moving averages *and* the 50 day moving average cross up through the 200 day moving average (the golden cross!). Now, once IJJP's price broke that orange line, it, in effect, was in a blue sky breakout. And as you can see, for about five months straight, IJJP ran straight up. But for actual charting purposes, there were four legs of the chart. See the white 10 day moving average line as it follows the price action? That line shows four major moves up, followed by a consolidation period where the price moved down a bit each time.

Price has a memory. IJJP saw a high price of $0.00065 and it saw it again. But on the second hit of that price, the buying pressure was so great that it busted through that level and went on to a new high of around $0.007. That's more than ten times your money.

Here is another chart example. This chart shows a previous high, again indicated by an orange line, however, that price point has yet to be broken. Here is the two year chart for PVSP:

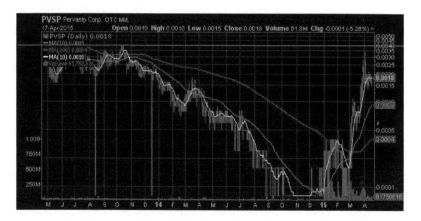

The orange line sows the previous high. As you can see, the price has climbed considerably for a few months, however, it has not yet hit that orange line. There is no telling whether or not it will actually hit that price, of about $0.004 price per share. But if it does and it breaks it, PVSP will then be in a blue sky breakout. But that price point is a major resistance level and will take a lot of buying pressure to push through it.

And again, you can see the price increase was preceded by both a 10 day moving average (white line) cross up through a the 50 day moving average (blue line) *and* the 50 day moving average cross up through the 200 day moving average (red line).

Although PVSP has yet to hit that previous high, this chart still shows that price has a memory. And even if PVSP doesn't hit that price point, there's still solid evidence based on this chart to support this first rule.

Two: People drive buying and selling

This rule is basically self-explanatory. But for the purpose of being thorough, I will say that without volume, there is no price action. The price will not increase or decrease if no one is trading it. Even if the market makers increase or decrease the bid or ask, if no one sells at the bid or buys at the ask, it will not matter. Therefore, people – or more specifically, traders – drive buying and selling.

We may only look again at the IJJP chart to see this fact. Here is the IJJP two year chart again:

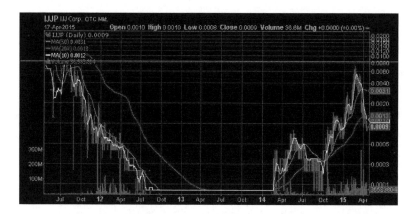

As you can see, when there was absolutely no volume, as is the case between before October 2013 and late May of 2014, there was absolutely no buying or selling and, subsequently, no price action.

IJJP may have had a cease order placed upon it by the SEC which would have frozen the trading of its stock and not allowed traders to trade it. I have not researched the reason for the lull in trading during that time. I only post this chart to prove the point that traders drive buying and selling and is represented by volume.

Once volume picked back up, the chart started to react nicely and the price increased.

Three: Buy at support and sell at resistance

This rule applies only to penny stock tickers whose chart clearly shows support and resistance levels. These charts are of those tickers that are trading in a channel or are on an uptrend with multiple legs.

A channel trading chart is one in which the bulls cannot break resistance and the bears cannot break support. Therefore, the price trades in a channel as it moves from support to resistance then back to support, etc…

An up trending chart with multiple legs is a chart that is in an uptrend and has clear consolidation periods. Without these consolidation periods, which are caused by traders taking profits, the chart will collapse under its own weight. This type of chart was described in "Penny Stock Players" for the ticker symbol REAC. REAC broke out and ran so hard that it collapse and crashed quicker than it increased. In fact, the entire breakout and collapse cycle happened in the span of a few hours.

To see an example of the uptrend with multiple leg chart, look no further than our previous THCZ chart:

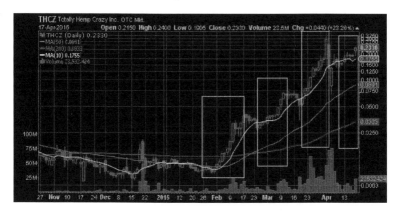

The yellow boxes show the green legs of an uptrend. In between the yellow boxes, are the red consolidation periods that absolutely *must* be present for a sustained uptrend.

To trade this chart, a smart prudent trader would buy at support and sell at resistance. Here are two charts for the ticker symbol IJJP which we have previously seen.

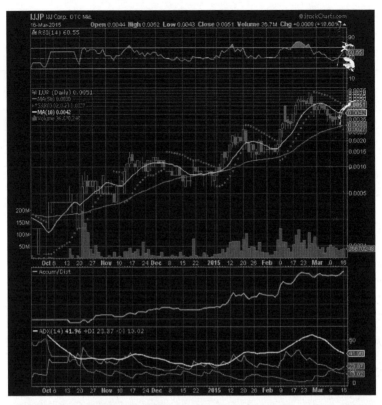

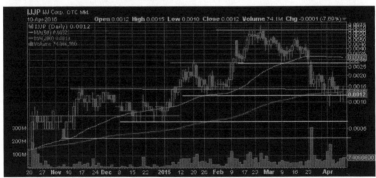

To explain these support and resistance levels and how to detect them, we must look at and analyze both of these charts simultaneously. But for the sake of simplicity, let's start with the top one.

The top chart shows a dotted red line that follows the price action. That dotted line is the Parabolic SAR (PSAR). As previously stated in chapter one, when the PSAR is above the price bars, it is considered bearish and the price is being pushed to the down side. And when the PSAR is under the price bars, it is considered bullish and the price is being pushed to the up side.

In early 2015, the PSAR flipped to the bottom. This flip coincided with the support level indicated by the yellow bar, third from the bottom at price point $0.0012. And on February 9th of 2015, there's another PSAR flip to the bottom which coincides with the orange bar which represents both a previous resistance and a current support level at the indicated date.

This means that the PSAR tells you when to buy and when to sell. When the PSAR flips to the bottom, you buy. When the PSAR flips to the top, you sell. And this is also confirmed when the PSAR flips line up with previous support and resistance levels.

However, once the chart is in a blue sky breakout, one must ignore resistance levels because they no longer exist. Therefore, pay attention to what the PSAR and other previously discussed indicators are telling you. Additionally, pay attention to support levels. If the newest previously developed support level falls, you should sell immediately. And if the chart rebounds, do not blame yourself for selling too early. And if it does not rebound, thank yourself for being a diligent and intelligent trader.

Now, back to consolidation. Without consolidation periods, you will see a chart like the following.

Here is the two year chart for the ticker symbol FITX:

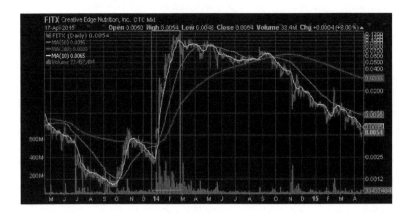

The orange box indicates the huge pump in early 2014 *without* any consolidation periods. And look what happened afterwards. The chart has been in a free fall because profit takers (bears) have taken over.

And price has a memory on the way down as well. So this ticker will probably see a price close to $0.0012 before the bears' takeover is stopped by the bulls.

And now to see an example of a channel trade. Here is the two year, very consolidated, MPIX chart:

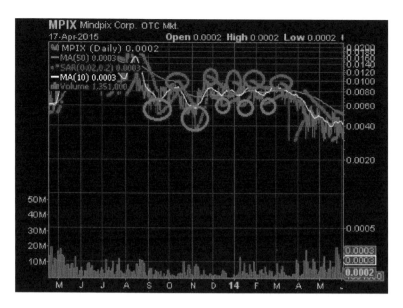

The green circles indicate buy points as dictated by the PSAR flip to the bottom. And the red circles indicate sell points as dictated by the PSAR flip to the top. If you traded this channel, you would have been afforded five trades, each with 100% or more gains. The channel traded from $0.005 to $0.01.

As previously stated, once support breaks, in this case the $0.005 level, you need to use other indicators to determine if you should buy back in. In this case, the 10 day moving average had begun to point down and never curled back up. So even though the PSAR flipped to the bottom, the support level was broken *and* the 10 day moving average showed a bearish outlook for the chart.

Four: Short rallies not sell offs

I will mention a few brief points about shorting a stock because shorting is not the focus of this book. You should never short a bottomed out chart. The point of finding bottomed charts is to buy long and ride the price up, then sell for the most profits.

When you short a stock, you are effactually borrowing shares of a company and selling them to the market at its current market price, then your desire is to buy them back later at a lower price. The difference in the sell and buy back price is your profit.

The risk of shorting a stock is majorly due to the fact that your broker can call your short whenever he or she wants. This is different than buying long where you can hold your shares for as long as you'd like. And furthermore, most trading platforms and brokers will not allow you to short a stock unless you have a margin account.

This margin account gives you the leeway of being wrong and still be able to afford to cover your position. Without enough funds in your account, there would be no way for you to pay for a losing short position that is called. Therefore, a margin account is desired.

You can do a simple Google search on shorting shares for a more in depth study. Or read my previously released book entitled "Penny Stock Manipulation".

Finally, in order to have a margin account, most brokers require a $10,000 minimum account. And to get to the point of rule number four, you should short a rally, which means that the price has climbed considerably. By shorting a rally, you catch the stock at the top and ride it down a few ticks to make your money. If you short a sell off, you risk catching the bottom and a substantial rally as traders try to buy the dip and push the price back up. If you get caught in a rally, you will lose the trade and your short position will cost you money.

*REMEMBER: Your broker can call your short position at any time and require you to close the short position, which may result in a sufficient loss of funds.

Five: Do not buy into a major moving average or sell into one

When a major moving average, such as the 50 day moving average or the 200 day moving average, is broken – either to the upside or the downside – the major moving average tends to act as support or resistance.

Therefore, if the price is moving up towards a major moving average, do not buy until it breaks and holds above it. Once the price breaks above and holds above the major moving average, that major moving average becomes support. In other words, if the major moving average is above the price, it is resistance. If the major moving average is below the price, it is support.

Therefore, if the trade reverses and moves against you towards the downside, and it is closing in – towards the downside – on a major moving average which is below the price, you should not sell unless that moving average is broken and the price does not immediately rally back up.

Additionally, if you are looking to enter a trade and the price is moving up and closing in on a major moving average towards the upside – the major moving average being above the price and acting as resistance – you should wait for the price to break above the major moving average and hold above it as confirmation before buying the stock.

These major moving averages, the 50 day moving average and 200 day moving average, are good barometers of support or resistance because of how long the price has traded above or below either of those averages.

To clarify, let's look at some charts.

Here is the daily chart for the ticker symbol BETS:

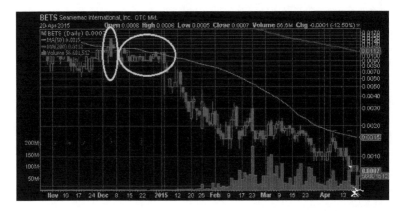

The line right above the price bars is the 50 day moving average. As you can see, it has acted as clear resistance for quite some time as the price never was able to penetrate it.

The first yellow circle shows that the price did break above the 50 day moving average, however, the break was never confirmed and the price dipped back down. A confirmation would be a candle like those described in chapter three. The best price candle for confirmation is the bullish engulfing candle.

The second yellow circle shows that the price touched the 50 day moving average but could never break it. This further confirms that this major moving average is resistance and you should not buy into it. *Always* wait for confirmation!

Here is an information packed chart. To make full use of what is going on with it, let's remember the reversal candles and confirmation candles that we discussed in chapter three (bullish engulfing, doji, hammer, shooting start, inverted hammer, hanging man).

Here is the daily MINE chart:

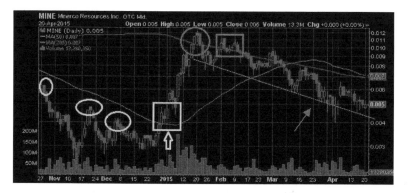

I know it looks busy. But I will clarify it all in a moment. First, look at the first three yellow circles (from left to right) that are below the blue 50 day moving average line. As you can see, these are highs and never really came close to the 50 day moving average.

However, the yellow arrow and yellow box indicates the break above the 50 day moving average. Inside the yellow box, you will see the candle that broke above the 50 day moving average, the red candle with a small body where profit takers tried to push the price back down but couldn't, *and* you will see the bullish confirmation candle to the right of the red candle, which is very close to bullish engulfing. That's your confirmation. If you did not buy the pure bottom, this would be your entry point at $0.004 to $0.005 price per share.

Now let's look up at the purple circle around the price bars at the 200 day moving average. Although the 200 day moving average is a resistance point, remember, never buy up into or sell down into a major moving average. Wait to see if the price breaks this point.

In this case, for MINE, the price did break the 200 day moving average. However, you immediately see the next candle as a hammer at the top, which is a reversal candle. And you see, immediately after that, confirmation of your sell signal as the price dropped considerably.

However, if you missed that sell point, you would then sell the first high inside the purple box that is at the 200 day moving average. Why? This will be explained when we discuss rule number eleven.

In the meantime, I'd like to point out a glaring obvious objection to the way I'm saying to trade this chart. That objection is the golden cross that occurred in mid-march.

This golden cross failed for two reasons. One, the chart was in a downtrend as indicated by the orange trend line that I've drawn for you (see the skinny blue arrow). And two, the volume was too low for the cross to be effective. Remember, without volume, there's no buying pressure. And without buying pressure, there is no price action.

Six: Do not chase momentum

As you can see, most of these rules tell you what not to do rather than what to do. As you learn to trade, you learn the things that you did wrong and therefore, these lessons are negative lessons that are derived from mistakes. Knowing what not to do is just as important, if not more important, than knowing what to do.

Rule six is do not chase momentum. This means that if a trader wants to buy into a stock but it is rising so fast that he cannot put hid buy order in at a reasonable price, then he should not buy it. If his buy order is getting rejected or just not filling because every time he puts his order in, the price jumps past it, then he would be wise and profitable to let the trade come to him.

Do not keep increasing a buy order price. Set the buy price and hope that the price dip hits that buy order and it gets a fill. Let's look at a chart example to see what I'm talking about.

Here is the SAPX chart:

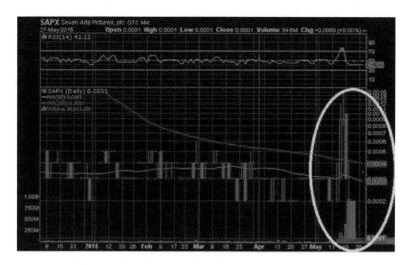

First of all, I know this chart is very choppy. So it is a risk to trade it. And normally, I'd advise against it. And for the purpose of bottom feeding, I'd still advise against it due to its inability to develop a trend.

However, as you can see, a lot of volume poured into this ticker. The price flew up. And if a trader got excited and bought this, she could be looking at catastrophic losses. Before the volume, SAPX was trading from $0.0002 to $0.0004 a share for a 100% flips. The volume pushed the price up to a high of $0.0015 a share.

If she bought this higher than $0.001 as she was chasing momentum, she would have seen a colossal loss after the third day of the pump. Remember the three day pump and dump rule? Never buy on the 3rd day! Those that did, could have gotten $0.0008 and sold $0.0015 depending on when each price actually hit. But that's a risk not worth taking.

Those that bought $0.0011 through $0.0015 per share of SAPX are now sitting at $0.0001 a share unless they cut their losses early. Traders who bought the bottom ($0.0002), could have gotten 6.5 time their money by selling at $0.0015. But again, gains like that are not worth it. These trades should only afford traders with an opportunity to buy low and ride momentum for a few hundreds of a percent max.

When pigs become hogs, they get slaughtered. Do not be a hog. Take profits and run or you will eventually get burned.

Do not chase momentum! And do not buy high on the 3rd day of a pump and dump.

Seven: Gaps get filled

What is a gap? A gap is when the price of a stock at the open is either higher than the previous close (gaps up) or lower than the previous close (gaps down). The space in between the close prices is the gap and it needs to fill at some point.

In other words, if a stock closes Monday at $0.02 a share and opens on Tuesday morning at $0.03 a share, there's a gap of a penny (between two and three cents) that needs to fill.

Gap ups are good if the trader buys the previous days close. But they are terrible if he is looking to enter the trade post the gap up. Do not buy a gap up! However, gap downs can afford a nice bounce provided that the gap down was not due to some substantial event within the company or the market itself.

If a stock closed at $0.02 on Monday and opened up at $0.03 on Tuesday, the gap needs to fill by coming back down to $0.02. It may not happen right away, but it will happen.

Let's take a look at a chart example of this. Here is the chart for ticker symbol PBMD:

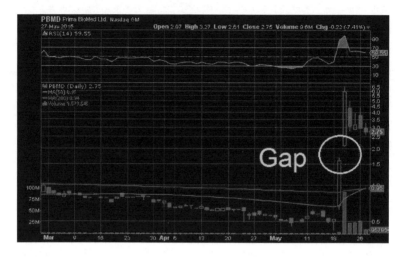

PBMD is already working towards filling the gap. That gap was a gap up and the price needs to come back down to around the $1.5 a share level. But once it does, and if volume is high, a new leg could form here.

Here is the ONCI chart which provides an example of a gap down:

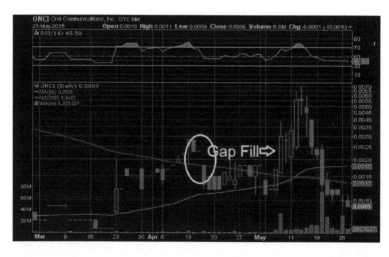

As you can see, there was a gap down in mid-April and it was filled in early May. Sometimes these gaps take a while to fill. But once it did, it exploded. Watch for bottoms post gap downs. But know that although gap ups fill, gap downs do not always fill. A trader can minimize his or her risk by waiting for the bottom to hit and for confirmation of a bullish reverse, which we've already extensively talked about.

Eight: Trends tests the point of previous support or resistance

A trend is the current direction of the price action of a particular stock ticker or index fund. Naturally, because index funds are a collection of stocks in a particular sector, they too have charts and trends.

Up trends occur when the price of a stock is increasing. Down trends occur when the price of a stock is decreasing. Sometimes, an uptrend can turn on a dime, although it is rare. Downtrends almost never turn on a dime. This will be delved into in much more detail when we describe rule number eighteen.

For now, let's talk about trends and how they work. Here is a previous chart that we described earlier for the stock ticker symbol PVSP:

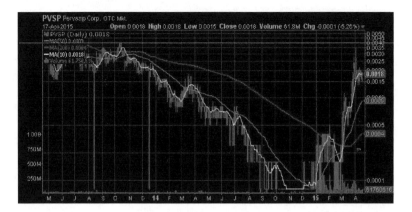

The orange line, as you can see, is the resistance line. The resistance line is the price that the stock was able to get up to (a previous price high) but could no longer sustain its bullishness. And, subsequently, the price fell.

In early 2014, PVSP reached the $0.004 price per share level. However, this was its ultimate high price and the trend turned down. However, in late 2014, after almost three months of stagnant trading, the price turned north into an uptrend.

As with before, the price tested close to the $0.004 level. Although the price never actually hit $0.004, it still proved to be a resistance point.

***NOTE: This PVSP chart, as far as reading price action is concerned, has everything we've talked about. Early in the chart, to the left, there was the bearish cross as the 10 day moving average crossed down into the 50 day moving average when it failed to push up through it. This failure of the 10 day moving average to push up through the 50 day moving average is due to two reasons. Reason one is that the price, as dictated by the market, was overpriced and over bought. Naturally, anyone can see that due to the downtrend that followed. Reason two is that there was almost no volume at all. Without volume, there is no price action. Other than the bearish cross, the price shows a down turn and proof that the downtrend almost never turns on a dime. The price didn't rebound for two years. In fact, once the bottom was in, it still took three months before an uptrend could form. The volume jus was not there. But once the volume poured in, the bullish 10 day moving average cross up through the 50 day moving average (did I mention this is my favorite bullish indicator?) quickly took root and the uptrend tree grew rapidly. Price reacted favorably as predicted by the cross. Then two months later, the golden cross hit with increased volume. In case you have forgotten, the golden cross is when the 50 day moving average crosses up through the 200 day moving average. The golden cross then proved to be extremely bullish.

To see a stock that is trying to turn from a downtrend, we will again visit a previously posted chart. Here is the FITX chart again:

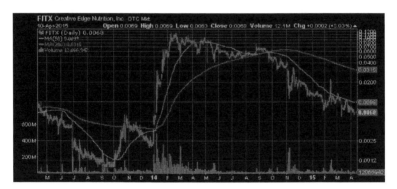

The high in late October of 2013 was a previous high. As you can see, the price climbed dramatically for months following the small dip after that high. The catalyst? Tons of news, volume, and a golden cross. Then, once the price completely topped at around 12 cents, FITX has been on a long downtrend. The price is slowly approaching that previous high that I mentioned in October of 2013 (a previous resistance level that had become a support level after the price broke it to the up side). If that support does not hold, FITX will see a crash to $0.0025. And if that price does not hold, less than $0.0012 price per share will be on the horizon.

Here is an annotated FITX chart:

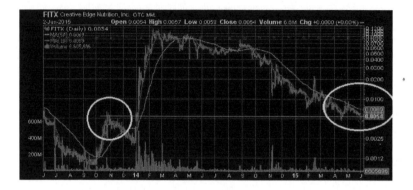

The yellow circle on the left denotes the previous high in October of 2013 as was previously mentioned. The yellow circle on the right denotes the current price *and* the fact that the price has bounced off the orange support line twice, although the first bounce occurred after the price dipped slightly below it. The orange line is the support which is the price the stock must test on its downtrend. As you can see, the line is drawn straight from the October 2013 high to the current price. So far, this price has acted as support and must hold for the stock to show its bullish strength as I tries to turn towards the upward direction. If this support level fails to hold, again, $0.0025 and $0.0012 are very high probabilities of price.

Nine: Trade with the tick, not against it

This rule is self explanatory. Basically, if a stock is upticking (increasing in price), traders want to buy long. They do not want to short an upticking ticker until the momentum runs out of steam. Also, if a stock is downticking (decreasing in price), traders do not want to buy long. They want to short a stock that is decreasing in price. And in this case, they are trading momentum and would not care as much about support and resistance, unless, of course, the price is already hitting one of those key levels. Traders would not want to automatically short a stock that is hitting support nor buy long a stock that is hitting resistance unless they are absolutely one hundred percent certain that momentum will carry them through those key price points.

A tick is the change in price from each trade. So an uptick will be a price that has increased from the previous price. And a downtick is when the price has decreased from the previous price. This does not mean that each tick is incrementally the same. A stock that has a spread of $0.01 on the bid and $0.02 on the ask will have a one cent tick. However, a stock that has $0.01 on the bid and $0.011 on the ask will have a one tenth of a cent tick.

This rule generally applies mostly to those who are high frequency traders who are trading large sums of money for small incremental gains. If a trader is of the mindset of trading a system based on his own guidelines and he is not looking for a few ticks of profit, then this rule only applies to him if he is trading a "trip" stock, such as those trading from $0.0001 and $0.0009 a share, because each tick gives him a high percentage of loss or gain. A trip stock is one that is trading with triple zeroes to the right of the decimal point, not counting trailing zeroes.

Ten: If the trader has to look, it is not there

This rule is also very self explanatory. Basically, this rule will save a trader when her brain tricks her into seeing something that really is not there. If she truly believes that something is not where she is looking, such as the salt shaker in a cabinet, then her eyes will deceive her and she will not perceive it even when she looks directly at it. Likewise, when she does want to see something very badly, her brain can trick her into seeing something that is not really there.

Examples of both of these are prominent in every day life. A lot of times the reticular activating system takes over. Have you ever noticed that when you buy a new car that all of a sudden you see them everywhere? But before, you never noticed them at all. That's the reticular activating system and it works on us all the time.

So if a trader learns a new indicator for stock chart reading and he then looks at a chart, initially if he does not see the new indicator, if he looks hard enough, his brain can actually make his eyes see it even if it truly is not there. So this rule is more of a caution. Do not go looking for indicators on a chart that, at first glance, are not there.

Also, sometimes it is beneficial to go away and take a break. Then to re-research a stock ticker with a different level of energy and frame of mind. Ever notice that when you want to find something, you never can? But then a few days later, when you no longer even care about the thing you were looking for, it automatically appears? And it usually does so in the very place you were looking. The same can be said about researching stocks.

Do not force the chart or the trade. Do not marry a stock. Let the trade come to you and if all of your indicators and research proves to be false, do not be afraid to escape that trade and take a loss. Everyone takes losses every now and then no matter how flawless his or her trading system.

***NOTE: It is also a common theme among traders that once we put in a ton of work into a stock ticker, we try to make it work. We do not want to lose the effort and time we just spent on a single company. Although this is reasonable as time is more valuable than money, it is also equally stupid. Do not lament doing your full due dilligence on a company and then deciding to walk away. Remember Warren Buffett's two main rules of investing, which can also be applied to trading: One, do not lose money. Two, see rule number one.

Eleven: Sell the second high, buy the second low

This rule is more complex than the previous two because it has two applications. The first application works during a trend. The second application works during the reversal of a trend.

First, during a trend, there are reversal chart patterns called "doubles". A double top is when a high is lower than the previous high and indicates that an uptrend is exhausting and a downtrend is about to ensue. A double bottom, on the other hand, is when there are two lows that are equivalent (or very close to being equivalent). But, a trader never knows when these reversals are going to hit. Therefore, it is wise to buy what we call "dips" which are when price decreases to a support level. Therefore, instead of buying a specific low and selling a specific high, a trader will buy a dip from a previous high, then sell the next high, rinse and repeat until the trend exhausts itself.

Second during a trend reversal, this is where the rule applies best. During a double top, you will see a high, then a second high that is lower than the previous one. Obviously, when a chart is topped, you would not buy. However, if you were lucky enough to grab the dip (first low in the double top) and sell the high (second high in the double top), then you would make a profit. However, once you recognize that pattern, it would be wise not to buy the second low because since the double top is a reversal pattern, the chart will more than likely fall into a downtrend. Likewise, during a double bottom, if you bought the second low and sold the second high, this would afford you protection against a failed uptrend attempt and give you profits.

Here is the chart for ticker symbol VMGI which shows a perfect double top where the second high is lower than the first:

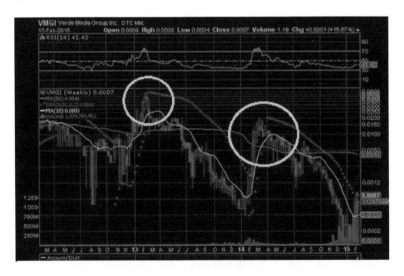

The yellow circles indicate the double top formation. But VMGI also shows a double bottom as well. In fact, $0.0001, which is VMGI's bottom, is the lowest a price can go. That's truly a bottom. However, the stock ticker had too much dilution and there were too many shares outstanding for the price to gain any steam off of the bottom. Traders were still able to muster enough momentum to increase the price to $0.0008 before it lost steam again. You can see this action if you look up the stock ticker.

But if a trader bought the first low at around $0.0005 and sold the second high at around $0.02, she would have received a nice return on investment. Additionally, if she bought the second low at $0.0001 to $0.0002 and sold the following high, which would have been the third high and not shown on this chart, at $0.0008, she would have also had a very nice return.

Twelve: The trend is the trader's friend in power hour

The trend is the trader's friend regardless of the time frame. But this is also true during what is commonly called the power hour. The power hour is the last hour of trading in a day. In Eastern Standard Time (EST), that means between three o'clock pm and four o'clock pm.

This, you will have to watch yourself on level II. Find a stock that has a lot of momentum, either bearish or bullish, and look at its level 2 in the final hour of trading. You will see that more often than not, except for bullish trends on day three of a pump and dump or on Fridays, that this trend will continue.

Fridays are notorious as sell off days because a lot of traders do not like to hold their positions into the weekend. This is intelligent if they are high frequency short term day traders because events beyond their control can cause the stock price to crash over the weekend. Bad news or initiated dilutive debt selling, also known as toxic debt, can trigger a selloff. In either case, retail traders such as you and I cannot sell their positions during closed business hours. Therefore, we risk losing a large chunk of our position in terms of money by having to chase to sell in a free fall if the news is so terrible that trader sentiment turns sour.

Fridays are not always a bad day and weekend holds can and are still profitable. But a trader should make sure her position is good before holding unless she is a long term holder to begin with and isn't concerned with the day to day trading. In the latter case, she has probably done all of her homework to make sure that her capital is as safe as possible. And if she is following a trading style that allows her to bottom feed, she is already positioning herself as close to the bottom as possible.

Another day that traders tend to be cautious on is Tuesdays. We call them "Terrible Tuesdays" as traders chase stocks that had a powerful increase in price per share on Monday and cut their losses on bad trades that they entered in on Monday.

Let's also not forget the three day pump and dump. That third day could be a cash crusher. So remember, do not chase a hugely pumped stock if it is on its third day of a pump and dump. Wait for the dip and catch the second wave of traders as they push the price back up.

To get back to the trend is your friend theme, watch level II on a stock that is on the first day or two of the pump on any day except Friday, and sometimes Tuesdays, and you will see a strong close. The trend, either bearish or bullish, will, more often than not, continue into power hour.

Power hour, in today's market, especially in penny stocks, can be more aptly named as power ten minutes. Nowadays, generally, a huge rush of buys do not tend to come in during the last hour, but they do in the last ten minutes as traders wait for the last second to buy in fear of a potential sell off, especially if the price has already risen dramatically.

If a bearish selloff is ensuing, expect that to continue in power hour. Trends in general do not tend to turn in the last hour except in the case mentioned above when a bullish pump and dump is on its third day or occurs on Fridays. Downtrends are not an exception. They also will continue to get sold into power hour.

In longer term trends, weeks to years, do not bet against the trend unless you are certain that it is reversing. See the information previously mentioned in his book to look for indicators that the trend is turning. All stars must be aligned and traders must receive confirmation signals before they can rest assured that the trend is reversing. Also remember that tops form faster than bottoms and so an uptrend will turn south quicker than a downtrend turns north.

Thirteen: Avoid the open

The open is the first half hour to one hour of trading. Yes, traders can make a profit by trading the open. But the volatility here is extreme and the trend can be deceptive. Unless the trader knows what is coming, it is too risky to trade the open.

The open will trick traders into thinking trading sentiment is either bullish or bearish until he or she buys in and then it will reverse. This isn't always true but often it is. Sometimes what happens in the open is the opposite of the actual trend of the day unless news is severely negative or positive and traders have gotten wind of it.

More often than not, vigilant traders will see that a stock that is up 100% in the first half hour of trading will end up closing down lower than the previous day's close. And that stocks that are down 50% during the open will often close higher than the previous day's close.

During the open, a trend has not been set and traders can be deceived in the above scenarios. So to be safe, avoid the open. Wait to see what the true trend is and then buy in. In fact, a trader can often watch the open for a dip in a stock price that he or she knows has no foundational reason for the dip, then buy in, and sell on the spike.

Of course, if you are trying to catch the bottom, there will be no reason to trade the open. Bottoms take a while to form and confirmation of a reversal of the bottom takes even more time. So this trading the open while bottom feeding is not just unreasonable but is also silly.

Avoid the open unless the open is your specialty!

Fourteen: Downtrends reverse after a top, two lower highs,
and a double bottom

The double bottom is the key here! Let's look at two charts
to see what this looks like. Here are the charts for IJJP
and PVSP:

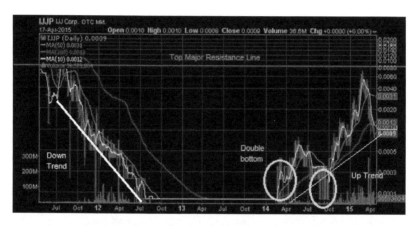

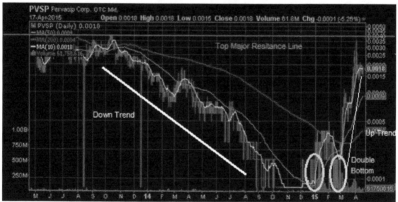

As you can see, the double bottom is very important. Do
not get faked out by the first top after the first bottom or
you risk both not buying the bottom and not buying into a
stock that is truly bouncing off of the bottom. Some
tickers do not bounce!

If you buy the first spike, you also risk having to take a loss if your trading system dictates that you do so. Never break your rules even if you are trying to buy the bottom. If your system dictates that you risk 20%, then sell at 20% *every* time. Naturally, if you are trading stocks in the $0.0001 – $0.0004 range, this rule would not apply as the lowest risk potential is 25%. However, you can still have a risk threshold for these trip stocks and adjust your rule accordingly. The key is to have the rule in place to protect yourself. So in effect, if you do have a 20% risk rule, you would either not trade stocks trading at $0.0004 and below or adjust your risk percentage to match a tick or two. So if you buy a stock at $0.0003 and it goes down one tick to $0.0002, that's a 33% loss. In that instance, . you can either decide that you were wrong and sell the stock for a 33% loss or adjust your risk potential even lower (66% loss) to $0.0001, or you can even just hold the stock until another flood of traders come in and push the price back up, if that even ever happens.

The main key is to know your risk tolerance, have a plan in place, and to watch for the double bottom and confirmation of a trend reversal before buying the stock. At least then, if you are wrong, you know you did your homework.

Fifteen: Bulls live above the 200 day MA, Bears live below it

To understand this better and to see it more clearly, let's start again by looking at a chart. Here is the daily chart for FITX:

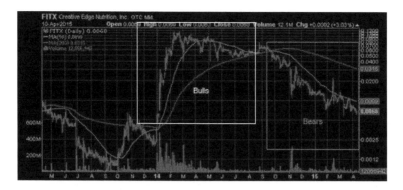

As you can see in this chart, the bulls kept the price increasing or sideways as long as it remained above the 200 day MA. However, once the 200 day MA was broken to the downside, the bears took over and a downtrend ensued.

Here, again is the IJJP chart:

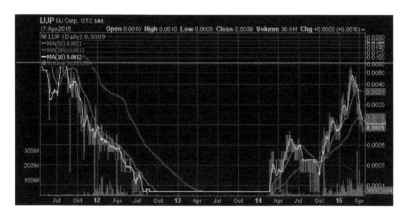

As long as price was below the 200 day MA (downtrend on the left part of the chart), the price was in a freefall. But once the 200 day MA was broken to the upside (right side of the chart), an uptrend took over.

So the 200 day MA can be used as a good barometer to tell traders if a true trend is in place, if the trend is not clearly seen otherwise.

Here is one more chart, since the rule is self-explanatory. Here is the PVSP chart:

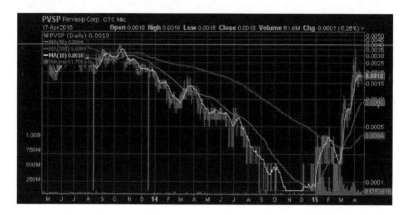

It's very easy to see the downtrend and uptrends and where the price action is relative to the 200 day MA.

Sixteen: Price has a memory

History repeats itself. We've seen in time and time again. A financial collapse happens, roughly, every 15-20 years. However, due to the increase in technology, especially in the financial industry, these financial collapses are going to happen at more frequent intervals. Instead of every 20 years, they are going to occur every 10 or so years, and then every 8 years, etc...

To say that these dips in the market are financial collapses is actually unfair. That's a media term that is thrown around to scare traders and investors away from the financial markets.

These "financial collapses" are actually just normal resets in the market. The world is not coming to an end and the economy is not failing. Everything that grows ends up collapsing. The same happens with the financial system. And in the case of the stock market, the growth of the indexes can only reach a certain level before the price must be reset. This is due to the finite about of money in the world and in the markets.

The old way of investing and holding your stock for 50 years and then retiring and selling your stock for retirement is dead. We are all financial traders in the 21st century. Therefore, we must now adapt to the ever changing, fast paced world of computer generated trading.

Thus, in order to take advantage of these resets every "X" number of years, depending on how advanced our system is and how quickly it moves, take a new way of thinking. We must become traders and no longer be traditional investors. That's not to say we can't hold a stock for 20 years. But it is to say that we must know when to sell our stock to maximize our profits and when to buy back in for maximum gain.

A reset in the market is coming. No one knows for sure when, but we can all rest assured that it is coming. The markets as of June of 2015 are so overbought that most of the indexes are soaring at unduly high levels. Almost every stock for a company is trading at a ridiculously high price, way above its intrinsic value.

Naturally, with a financial market such as the stock market, where investor or trader money pushes the stock price up at an exponential rate when compared to the stock price if only net assets were calculated, the stock price should be higher than its intrinsic value. But since that is the case, the reset, when traders start taking their profits, can cause what seems like a financial collapse. But these traders will buy back in at price levels they are comfortable with and push the price back up. So have no fear. The stock market will not completely crash. The lure of a huge financial gain with, although much effort, not much work is too great for the gambling nature of human beings to avoid.

The good news is that we traders who trade penny stocks do not have to worry about all of that. Penny stocks do not, in general, trade with the markets. They have a life of their own. But, like the stock market, they do have price memory.

If the price has hit a low level once before, at some point in time, it will hit that level again. Likewise, if a stock price has hit a high level once before, it will eventually hit that price again.

Here is the chart for the ticker symbol MINE as an example:

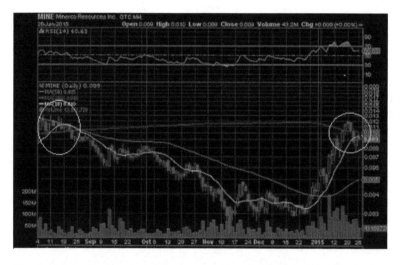

The left circle shows the previous price high and the right circle shows that it hit this price again. It took a while, but the price eventually did hit the high.

Sometimes this rule can mislead you. Sometimes the price comes very close to the previous price but does not quite hit it. This is where being a vigilant and intelligent trader comes into play.

Here is the chart for ticker symbol PVSP:

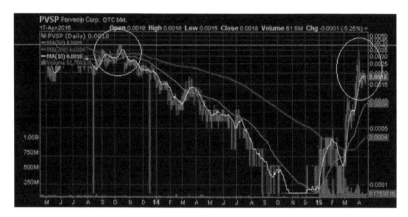

As you can see, the price came very close to but did not touch the previous high. So just know that, although price still has a memory, chart reading is an art and not an exact science.

Seventeen: Big volume kills moves by causing the ticker to trade sideways

But I thought we want a lot of volume? We do! In the beginning, we want as much volume as possible. But over time, with constant days of high volume, the ticker will end up in a channel because there will be equal number of shares being bought as there are being sold.

This rule is a misnomer in the sense that any amount of volume can cause a ticker to trade sideways as long as there is equal buying and selling. The volume does not have to be high. However, if the volume is high, it will cause a trend to be formed. Then if the volume stays high for any length of time, the trend will then turn sideways into a channel. Then traders must hold and wait for the channel to be broken either to the upside or the downside.

So be cautious about buying into a ticker with consistent volume, even if it is in a trend.

Eighteen: Trends never turn on a dime

Take a look at any of the preceding charts and you will see this in action. Downtrends have to form a bottom in order to reverse and that takes time. And uptrends must form a top in order to reverse and that also takes time.

Also, once a trend starts to turn, there are always traders who try to reverse it before the new trend takes root. So if a stock is in an uptrend and a top is formed, there will usually be another spike in price at the beginning of the down turn before the true downtrend forms.

This also applies to stocks in the down trend. Hence the double bottom. There will always be traders who try to push the stock back down after a short spike before the true uptrend forms off the bottom.

Nineteen: Bottoms take longer to form than tops

Again, take a look at the preceding stock charts and this will be a fact that jumps out at you. Tops form very quickly. But bottoms tend to take months and years to form. This is due to the fact that buyers get wary about buying the top so the price increases get exhausted fairly quickly. However, the formation of bottoms include buyers and sellers alike slowly getting a feel for the way the chart is trading.

Also, the increased price tends to happen rapidly. But the decrease in price happens slowly over time for the very reason explained in the previous paragraph. It is only natural that what happens quickly also fizzles quickly.

As an analogy, have you ever taken pre-workout or a massive amount of caffeine only to have a crash afterwards come on out of nowhere? It's the same concept except the crash in the stock price does not happen as fast as the crash after a caffeine binge. The quicker the increase in price, the sooner the top forms, and the sooner the downtrend begins. So be careful of stock prices that jump up rapidly in price, especially those that do so for no apparent reason. It is safer to miss an insane increase in price than it is to jump in and risk buying the top. If you must trade a stock that is soaring in price, see rules three and eleven. Buy the dip!

Twenty: Beat the crowd into and out of the door

This is the old adage, buy low and sell high. By following the guidelines of this book and forming your own rules, you will be able to do this effortlessly. You do not have to beat everyone into the door by buying before you have confirmation of a formed uptrend, but you must beat most of the traders (the crowd) into the door.

Likewise, you do not have to beat every trader out of the door, but you must get out before the crowd gets out. This is timed by having a system. Bottom feeding allows you to catch the bottom of the stock price. However, traders should still have a system for a certain percentage gain to sell. And traders should sell at this percentage every time. Or if you have another system that works for you, that is fine. But stick to your system and do not deviate.

Trading System Trick: Make your downside percentage risk half that of your desired upside potential gain. If you want 50% profit, do not risk losing more than 25% as your loss. By trading in this fashion, you can lose more often than you win and still be profitable...to a point.

Chapter 10 – Conclusion

Wow, that's a lot of stuff, huh? Let's recap what we have learned in this book. And remember, you may read this as many times as you'd like. Take the information that you find valuable and disregard the rest. Life, and trading, is about being a student not a follower. That is something I first realized when I heard a Jim Rohn speech.

Also, before we recap, remember that this book, like all the Penny Stock Players books are intended as guidelines to point you to the path of knowledge so that you can be a great and successful trader. Some things may not resonate with you and that is okay.

The things that we have covered are, first, the momentum indicators. We learned about the On Balance Volume line, the Accumulation/Distribution line, the Parabolic SAR, and the AD line with +DI and –DI. We learned what they are, how they work, and how to trade them.

Next, we learned about volume and the moving average, specifically the 10 day moving average, the 50 day moving average, and the 200 day moving average.

In Chapter 3, we learned about the Relative Strength Index and the candle formations and how to trade them. We learned about reversal candles and confirmation candles.

In Chapter 4, we learned how to put all these indicators and candle formations together to read the chart and find the bottom.

In Chapter 5, we learned about the pump, how it works and how to trade it.

In Chapter 6, we learned how to look up financials and the share structure. We also learned how to compare different priced stock tickers to find low floats.

In Chapter 7, we learned about news and press releases and how they affect the stock price. We learned how to find the news and press releases and how to watch the stock price and chart to determine trader sentiment.

In Chapter 8, we learned about momentum and how to trade with the crowd. But more specifically, we then learned that we should find these momentum trades before they become momentum trades so that we can get in and out before the crowd.

And finally, in Chapter 9, we learned how to interpret the trading rules and guidelines that the student learned from the Mayor board and used as his northern star as he navigated the trading seas.

Before we move on to the bonuses, my challenge to you is to learn as much as you can about this game. And if you are a trader and are not yet successful, do not give up. Open a paper trading account and make sure you practice, practice, and PRACTICE! I cannot stress the need for experience enough.

Additionally, have the courage to trust your trading system in real money once you realize that is works with paper trading. Never deviate from your system or you risk losing all. Also, make sure you speak with a financial and trading professional before dropping a dime in the market. Most will advise you against trading penny stocks. But again, this is your game and we traders should realize that and be a student. Don't just do what others tell you to do.

This goes for other traders too who are alerting stocks. Do not buy something just because someone tells you to. Put it through your litmus test and make sure it passes your rules. If it does not, do not trade that stock. And do not beat yourself up mentally or emotionally if you choose not to trade a stock and it sours to 300% gains. Remember, it is better to miss a huge percentage gain than it is to lose 100% because you are in such a hurry to trade a stock.

And if you have to take a loss, do yourself a favor and take a few days off from trading. The emotional feeling you have after taking a loss may make you do something stupid like buy a stock with un-cleared funds. Trust me, take the time off! Let your emotions cool down. Re-read this book or read your own guidelines, which, by the way, should be on a sticky note on your computer and hanging on your refrigerator.

Once you've established a consistently winning method, write it down to the T. Stick it on your fridge or computer and read it daily. Never forget your rules. Make it a check list that you have to check off with every stock that you want to trade and if the rules are not satisfied, then do not trade that stock.

It's okay to be wrong and to take a loss. If you are successful with paper trading but when you trade with real money it doesn't work out, then go back to paper trading. Sometimes we are more daring with money that is not real and, thus, we can take more risks and through the numbers game, we win more often. And when we start trading real money, we are more cautious and are afraid to pull the trigger due to self-doubt. That's okay too and will pass over time as we win on more trades.

And do not be afraid of adjusting your trading style or amending your rules. But do this slowly. Make sure it is the right move. Do not constantly change your rules from day to day. This is not having rules at all.

And learn as much as you can. Use this book as a finger pointing to what is important and go out and seek more information. And remember too, these rules can be applied to blue chip stocks as well, not just penny stocks.

Good luck with your trading and I hope to hear from you in the future as a very successful and prosperous stock trader.

Bonus 1: Resources

For more on candles:
http://www.candlestickshop.com/glossary/#Hammer
(Bullish)

For more on valuing:
http://www.BuffettsBooks.com

http://www.GuruFocus.com

For more on charting:
http://www.BarChart.com

http://www.StockCharts.com

For more on paper trades:
http://www.smartstocks.com

For more on research:
http://www.DDAmanda.com

http://www.MarketWire.com

For more on message boards:
http://www.ihub.com

http://www.InvetorsHangout.com

http://www.TheLion.com

Your best friends:
http://www.YouTube.com

http://www.Google.com

http://www.Facebook.com

http://www.Twitter.com

Bonus 2: Chapter 2 of my book "Penny Stock Players" entitled: Beginner Trading

The Student bought his first stock ever via an internet trading platform (TradeKing) at one dollar and five cents per share. He was just learning what he was doing. So he realized that buying only 10 shares with a commission of $4.95 an order would not net him any profits unless the stock he bought jumped to roughly one dollar and ninety cents a share. This would give him a dollar profit. Nonetheless, he bought this stock anyway just to get the experience.

The stock he bought, CYTK, climbed to one dollar and nine cents a share in roughly two months. The Student decided to sell this stock just before he transferred his account to Etrade. He just got so frustrated because TradeKing had a limit on pink sheets and over the counter stocks. TradeKing blocked most trading in these low priced stocks due to what they called "unforeseen trade charges that could run in the thousands of dollars". So he was unable to trade most of what he wanted, which were stocks under a penny. What a joke!

Pink sheet stocks (PK) and over the counter stocks (OTC) are stocks that do not trade in a common stock exchange, such as the NASDAQ or New York Stock Exchange (NYSE), among others. Therefore, before transferring his account to Etrade, The Student went ahead and bought a few shares of Disney (DIS) and Birkshire Hathoway (BRK.B) because he was able to trade for $4.95 a trade with TradeKing, while Etrade charges $9.99 a trade. Then he called Etrade and sent in the necessary documents in order to get his account fully transferred to Etrade. The entire process took about a week and a half.

Now that his account was fully transferred, The Student was ready to get into his penny stock trading business. Through talking to a few people about his interest, he found out that one of his friends, The Doctor, also traded stocks. So, they started exchanging information and philosophies. The Doctor's philosophy was to jump in at the open on a stock that is soaring and to ride it until he felt ready to sell. However, avoiding the open is something that The Student soon learned was wise to do.

Unfortunately for him, The Student's penny stock trading business, like many other startup businesses, lost money. Initially, he traded with his friend, The Doctor, by buying a stock at the open. However, because he was new at the volatility of these penny stocks, he let his emotions take control of him and he sold at the worst of times.

His first month of trading was in April. During this time, he lost 20% on FITXD, 18% on HIDC, 98% on LBTG, 58% on PUNL, 27% on AMBS and 29% on REVI. He lost all these percentages by buying in as the stock was soaring and watching it immediately reverse its fortunes. Later, The Student learned that all of these stocks were paid promotions and that he should have never bought into them.

During this time, however, he happened to find a message board on ihub.com called The Mayor Board. Before he actually let down his defenses and trusted the board, he actually put it on his ignore list, especially The Mayor. On the ihub's main page, there is a twitter feed which reposts all messages that are posted on respective boards. The Mayor Board was one of those boards. The Mayor's posts were one of the main posts that were tweeted on this twitter feed. So The Student naturally thought that The Mayor was just pumping his own stocks. He later found this to be the most unwise deduction that a person in his position could have made.

Because of The Mayor and the Board, during this month of April, even though he lost a total of $300.00 on his trades, The Student was still up $80. And this is how: since The Student was a newbie, he knew he was going to lose money in the beginning. So he only funded his account with $1200. First he deposited $500, then anther $300 and then finally another $400 was added as he continued to lose money. However, each trade that he made was no more than $150.00 per stock. Although trading in such small amounts makes it harder to lose money, it also makes it harder to make money. At a hundred dollar buy in, the stock, at $9.99 per trade (let's say ten dollars to make it simple and that's ten dollars to buy and ten dollars to sell), a stock would have to rise 20% just to break even. Even in the penny stock world, 20% does not always happen right away nor does it always go in the buyer's favor, which is something The Student learned the hard way.

Now, onto The Mayor and the Board's saving grace; there were three plays which The Mayor alerted to his Mayor Board that made The Student money and kept him out of the red. Red means actually losing money. These stocks were REAC on which he made 121%, MPIX on which he made 49% and TDEY on which he made 115%. And this brought his grand total to positive eighty dollars, meaning $80 in the green.

Unfortunately for The Mayor, there were many attackers on ihub who accused him of being a pumper. Once a penny stock rises to hundreds and thousands of a percent, it is bound to get exhausted and collapse. This very situation happened to REAC. It ran up to about 130% (.03 PPS) and then within minutes it crashed all the way down to .01 PPS, only to settle at about .014 PPS. Those that bought high thinking it would keep going up, chastised those who initially alerted the stock ticker. The

Student himself had been a victim of this penny stock volatility. But not this time; he got out almost right at the top. So he was beginning to learn the game.

REAC was the stock ticker which provoked The Student to call the The Mayor Board home. But not every alert made him money. The Student still had a long way to go before he truly learned the game. He felt like he learned a lot. He knew how to read level II (L2), which shows how many shares were being bid and for what price and how many shares are being sold on the ask and for what price. He also knew how to read charts and interpret technical analysis. But somehow, he missed one of the most crucial pieces to penny stock trading.

Bonus 3: Chapter 5 of my book "Market Manipulation" entitled: Market Makers

The market is starting to turn towards the way of the United States currency system. John Law in the late 1600s into the early 1700s was a Scottish economist. What Law believed and instituted was what is now called fiat currency. Fiat currency is a currency that has no intrinsic value. All currency in a fiat system is just a medium of exchange.

Today, in the 21st century, the United States is now on the fiat currency system. There used to be gold in Fort Knox to back up the paper and coin money. So if you ever wanted, you could go to the treasury and ask for gold in exchange for your money. That system has since been abolished and there is not enough gold to cover the amount of printed money.

In fact, before the invention of fiat currency, money, especially coins, were made from metals that had its own intrinsic value. These coins were made from gold, silver, copper and other precious metals that, if needed, could be melted down and used in or for utilities.

These precious metal coins in previous societies were "watered down" with other metals to save the treasury money. However, the citizens eventually caught on to their tricks because the coins eventually became basically worthless and merchants would stop accepting them as payment. In this way, every fiat currency and "watered down" currency has failed.

I'm not saying the United States currency system is going to fail nor am I trying to undermine your confidence in American money. However, to understand what is now happening in the stock market, you must first understand what has happened to our money. We are no longer under the gold standard. Our money, except for the coins, is paper with which we can do nothing except use as a medium of exchange.

Furthermore, our money system is now becoming an electronic system. No precious metals, nor paper money, are being exchanged much anymore. Think about it. When you get paid and have direct deposit, it is now just electronics that say you have X number of dollars deposited into your account. But there are no actual dollars. It's all lights and on off switches. The same thing happens when you take money out of an ATM. Sure you get paper money out of it, which is intrinsically worthless, but your account is still controlled by electronics.

This is the system that stocks have basically gone to. Take a look at the exchange floor that used to be buzzing with life and had hundreds of people yelling at each other and writing things down. Now, there are just a handful of these people on the floor. The stocks are not being traded in person anymore.

We traders now have the power to trade our stocks at home on our computer. It's all electronic. We do not need to go to a broker anymore. Trades can be made for as little as $4.99 a trade. We have no true limit to the number of trades we make as long as we have cleared funds. But with this great power comes considerable risk.

Think about that now. Your trades are no longer going through or being approved by a person. It's all computerized. What does that mean? The market is now manipulated by a computer. Sure, there are algorithms and such that have been programmed by humans, but there is a real sense of artificial intelligence that takes the algorithms and controls the price of the stock. Not every block on L2 is necessarily someone selling anymore. It could be the computers controlling the price, knowing that people will buy at that price. And until the trading volume changes, there is no reason to really change the bid or ask.

Have you ever placed a bid above the current bid only to have your bid not show up on L2? Have you ever placed a sell order on the market to have the price hit but your sell order not fill? It makes you think.

Additionally, these computers make trades in milliseconds and can buy or sell hundreds of shares before you can even place your order. Plus, they see you coming and can manipulate the price once they see your order is placed.

I know that this is sounding like some conspiracy theory, and maybe it is. However, I don't think it is far-fetched that a system that is based on computers is not, in some way, manipulated by those computers.

Market makers can trade stocks at whatever price they wish without the public's consent. Have you ever seen an oddball trade? For example, a company will trade between 20 cents and 30 cents throughout the day, then there will be this strange trade at 4 cents. Do you honestly think someone will actually sell their shares at such a cheap price? This oddball trade can be high too. In this example, a trade of 50 cents or more would be made. Why would anyone buy a stock for 50 cents a share when he or she can get it at 30 cents a share?

***NOTE: An outlier trade can also be a trader who accidently put a decimal in the wrong place. But one would have to wonder, is this trader really not looking at the amount of money the trade is costing? A simple check of the price of the buy or sell should alert a trader of his or her mistake. Unless, of course, he or she got the shares wrong too. To which I say, you really should find something else to do with your money. But hey, a least they put sell when they meant to sell and buy when they meant to buy, right? Let's give credit where credit is due.

After market trades, often referred to as T-trades, can reflect the wrong close price. Then there's the occasional error, either someone putting a decimal in the wrong place or the trade going through wrong on the other end. Here's a prime example of an error or T-trade that was entered wrong:

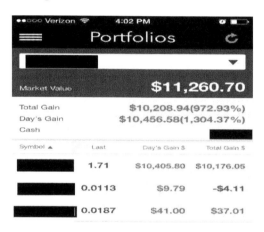

Then there are the consistent prints of 10,000 share trades. This is just market makers trading to each other. No big deal, I know. But why would market makers do that unless they were trying to keep the price of the stock at a certain range?

Other ways the market makers manipulate the trades is through pre-market trading, post-market trading, and hiding shares on level 2. When the market closes, it only closes to the public. Others can still trade. So the close price we see is not always the close price. That is how we get gap ups and gap downs (when the price opens higher or lower than it closed).

Share hiding is something that market makers love to do. Have you ever noticed that, on level 2, you will see 10,000 shares on the ask at a certain price. Then once those shares are bought, another 100,000 shares will all of a sudden show up? There's no way that someone immediately just put in a sell order of 100,000 shares. Those shares were already being sold, however, the market makers decided not to show them.

Here is an L2 example:

Symbol	Last Trade	$ Chg.	C...	% Chg. C...	High	Low	Volume	Exchang...	Last	Size
	0.0002	-0.0001		-33.33	0.0003	0.0001	208,93...	V	0.0002	3500000
									12:54:30	
									0.0001	100
MMID	Bid		Size		MMID	Ask	Size		12:48:12	
CANT	0.0001		10K		VFIN	0.0002	10K		0.0002	100
CSTI	0.0001		10K		ETRF	0.0002	9048K		12:47:09	
FANC	0.0001		10K		NITE	0.0001	8518K		0.0001	100
ATDF	0.0001		5010K		ATDF	0.0006	1355K		12:45:27	
VFIN	0.0001		10K		CSTI	0.01	10K		0.0002	100
ETRF	0.0001		15998K		FANC	0.01	10K		12:43:13	
NITE	0.0001		851959K		CDEL	0.0157	10K		0.0001	100
					CANT	0.25	2500		12:42:05	
									0.0002	100
									12:41:26	
									0.0001	100~
									0.0002	1417500
									0.0002	41250

As you can see, VFIN is showing 10,000 shares of this ticker at $.0002. But for anyone who knows anything about VFIN, they know that there is no way that is all the shares that VFIN has. Additionally, look at the trades on the right. 100 shares at $.0001 is a penny and 100 shares at $.0002 is 2 cents. Who in their right mind would buy or sell for 2 cents or less when trades themselves cost at least $4.99? Simply put, that is market maker manipulation via computer trades, often called paper or print trades.

The most common market makers who hide shares are VFIN, VNDM, NITE, and BRKT.

Then there's the share shifting that happens. In level 2, shares on the bid or ask will often flash and then disappear. Sure, there may be traders who set a bid or a sell order and then change their mind almost immediately. But when this happens multiple times in a few seconds on the same ticker, it makes you wonder what is really going on there.

Trading hasn't changed much since we've gone to the computer based system. Traders still have confidence and they should. Traders play the volatility of a stock and investors look for the long term. With the former, we want prices to fluctuate so we can make some profits. With the latter, we want stable increases in a growing company and we are not necessarily concerned with making money in the short term.

As long as the market system works and there is volatility where there should be and there is stability where there should be, we should continue to trade as we normally would. But we should also be informed of the type of organization that we are dealing with; only then can we make intelligent decisions with our trades.

Of course there has to be public traders trading a stock in order for the market makers to have a reason to manipulate it. Public traders are our next discussion of manipulators.

But before we move on, we must first discuss a topic known as Naked Shorting.

Naked Shorting

Naked shorting is why press releases, news, and financials will never make a difference on OTC companies. The investor always gets burned as a long term holder. Stocks in the OTC are trades based on momentum. Again, I reiterated, do not put more money into a penny stock than that which you can afford to lose. Market makers are allowed to do what I'm about to describe and it is called naked shorting and is a corrupt form of trading.

There is a rule that allows market makers to do what is called naked shorting. The rule allows the market makers to create as many shares as they need in order to uphold a well-ordered market system.

Here is a direct quote from this rule: "Proprietary short sales No member shall effect a short sale for its own account in any security unless the member or person associated with a member makes an affirmative determination that the member can borrow the securities or otherwise provide for delivery of the securities by the settlement date. This requirement will not apply to transactions in corporate debt securities, to bona fide market making transactions by a member in securities in which it is registered as a Nasdaq market maker, to bona fide market maker transactions in non-Nasdaq securities in which the market maker publishes a two-sided quotation in an independent quotation medium, or to transactions which result in fully hedged or arbitraged positions."

The rule allows a market maker to create shares in a company by simply taking the money from the purchaser and making an electronic entry into their brokers' account, and the broker then electronically credits the buyer with the exact number of shares of that company. But some things that most are unaware of take place in this transaction.

First, the purchaser or trader thinks that his shares actually exist, but unless he or she has read his trading account's full agreement very carefully, he won't understand the true nature of the transaction and that all he or she really did is give money to a broker or someone else other than the company, and never got any actual proof of ownership. The trader's real proof of purchase is, seemingly, sitting at the DTCC.

Second, the market maker filling the order for the shares has the trader's real money, and gave nothing except an electronic receipt acknowledging this fact. Another very important aspect to understand is that at no point in this transaction did the company in which the trader 'invested' ever get even a penny of the money that was paid. There is a major misunderstanding that causes traders to assume that when they buy a share of a company's stock, the company actually gets the cash.

This is only true if the trader is buying an IPO, or a private placement of shares from the company. In any other purchase of a stock by a trader, the company does not see the money from the trade. This is most puzzling when a trader begins to understand what happens during naked shorting. Often, the circumstances where the provision that allows for naked shorting to maintain an orderly market is actually abused and is used to manipulate the market. Whoever is doing the naked shorting is the entity that is actually receiving the money.

And they are allowed to keep it for as long as they'd like. This is where the manipulation of the rule take effect. The rule was originally created to allow the market makers, who by becoming such an entity, agree to create a market in particular stocks. This means that they can sell you shares, or buy shares from you, even if there isn't any actually available.

The main market makers' goal is to provide liquidity in the market. In securities with a small float, the market makers' ability to naked short is vital to the liquidity of that security. Market makers abuse this authority when they determine that the market for a particular security has become too unsystematic. Far too great of buying pressure, for example, can cause a price to increase precipitously to the point that it has no relationship to the true book value of said security.

The market maker then decides that he will naked short the stock in order to fill orders, knowing that by doing so, the price will not explode due to remarkably high demand. And the market maker can literally issue new shares under this rule. The market maker then waits, with an open naked short position in that stock, until the buying pressure diminishes. Then he can buy back shares at lower price in order to cover his naked short position. The rule does not have any time constraints and that allows for the market maker to keep a naked short position open for as long as he'd like. In reality, his position simply stays open, and the money stays in his account until the buying pressure is gone.

There is another provision of this rule that states that the market makers do not have to publish their open naked short positions, ever! All penny stock (pink sheet) securities can be naked shorted, indefinitely, by market makers, and there is no way that a trader can find out if in fact there is an open naked short position in a stock he is trading. So far, the SEC has not appreciated a strong need to correct this type of trading.

There are unlimited amounts of shares that were never authorized by the company made available to the unsuspecting investor or trader. However, they are authorized and issued by the market makers and protected by this rule.

This is why the lure of abusing this rule is so great: if a million naked shorted shares are issued and sold by a market maker at .001 (one tenth of a cent), that equals $1,000 that the market maker keeps in his account. At

.01 (one cent), the market maker gets to keep $10,000. Now, that is for each million shares that the market maker creates. The price of the stock then decreases or trades in a channel, even though there is insanely increased levels buying.

The company often suspects that there is someone illegally shorting their stock in an attempt to sabotage them. The shareholders think that the company is illegally printing shares or unloading the shares without informing them. Eventually, the distrust between the company and its shareholders becomes so immense that traders start selling. Additionally, the company, already damaged by a decreased share price, is forced to issue additional shares into the market by increasing their Shares Outstanding because loans cannot be taken out due to decreased market cap caused by the decrease in share price. In both cases, the market maker is afforded the opportunity to cover his short position.

Bonus 4: The Student's 2015 Trading Experience:

The Student started off 2015 by depositing $250.00 into his account. He has never been afraid of a challenge and he wanted to see if his system still worked. He had been out of the game for over six months. Things change over time as we all know.

Through the power of this system and the patience of a Zen master, he increased his trading capital to $2,000. He traded stocks such as VDRM, IJJP, PVSP, SAPX, VMGI, BETS and THCZ for nice gains.

But he also took his share of losses on stocks such as ECIG, BLDV, and BETS.

The year started off great as the Student traded VDRM for 100% profit with a buy in of $150.00, which brought his total to $380.00 after trade fees. Not a bad start to the year.

Then someone messaged him on Facebook, for the second time, asking him to buy a stock at an inflated price. The guy who messaged him said that he'd then buy the same ticker at a ridiculously inflated price. When the Student ask the guy why he would do that, he simply replied "because I like to help people".

Really? No way was the Student going to fall for some crap like that. Maybe in the very beginning when he didn't know what he was doing. But he has become way more intelligent of a trader to fall for that mess.

That guy probably bought the stock at a higher price and just wanted out. As soon as the Student bought the ticker, he'd be out because his shares were probably the ones on the ask.

If you are a newbie, do not fall for that trick. Never buy a stock as a favor for another trader. You may find friends in this game. But when it comes to money, people look out for themselves.

Next, the Student took a 50% loss on ECIG with a $200.00 buy in. ECIG was a fellow trader's recommendation and the Student knew that it didn't fully satisfy his rules. But he bought it anyway and paid the price. I cannot stress enough that traders should always stick to their rules and guidelines. So then the Student was down to $270.00 and that's when things took off.

IJJP and THCZ were amazing buys for him. They both passed his litmus test to the T and afforded him amazing gains. They both allowed him multiple gains of 50-100%. And before he knew it, he was sitting on $1300.00.

This money he put to good work as he entered VMGI. This stock afforded him multiple trades from $0.0005 to $0.0008 a share, each time he would remove his original position and retain free shares. The final trade caused him to have to take a loss here though as there are just too many shares and not enough volume for the ticker to really take off. The chart looked promising though for an uptrend that just never gained steam.

That was the peak of the Student's year. He was sitting at $2182.57 and then came BETS and BLDV. The former, he took a loss of 50% and then bought back in for a nice profit before exiting BETS for good. The latter, BLDV, turned out to be a stinker. The company has promise but the Student bought at the wrong time.

He bought BLDV at $0.0006 a share and had to sell $0.0001 because of two reasons. One, he did not follow his rules again and held onto the shares even though they hit a 50% loss. And the reason he ended up selling is because BLDV announced they were going to perform a reverse split. This news is what caused BLDV to fall quickly in price. And, instead of having a 50% stop loss in price, by the time the Student read the news, the price had already dropped precipitously.

A reverse split is not always bad. But it is in the Student's rules to never buy into one. If the split already happened, a prudent trader would watch for the dip and buy the bottom. These companies that do a reverse split often see huge gains after the split and dip. But the Student did not want to risk having his money in a reverse split just in case the stock price got watered down afterwards.

After the BLDV debacle, the Student caught SAPX on a momentum trade. It was a pure pump and dump and he got in on the second day of the pump and sold at the top on the third day of the pump for a 60% gain.

But the Student soon realized that summer time trading, as opposed to spring and fall, is a completely different animal. Many penny stock traders pull their funds during the summer. So the moves in penny land are more sporadic. But the ones that run, run hard. A trader may only look at THCZ and IJJP to see an example.

So the Student, for the time being, pulled most of his penny stock trading funds and sent them home. He left a few hundred dollars in the account just in case he finds that hidden gem.

But the Student still trades blue chips. He has an account with Trade King for that purpose as he uses E-Trade for penny stock trading. He heard from a wise trader once to never mix your speculation with your investments as the temptation to sell your investments and put the money into speculation is far too great due to the lure of incredible gains.

And as he learns time and time again, the potential for incredible gains comes with the risk of demoralizing losses.

The Student still came out on top with a profit of close to $800.00 in penny stocks. He will re-enter the penny stock game full-time again in the fall. In the meantime, he was able to catch MJMJ and ARYC for over 100% each. And he had a bid in MDCN at $0.0012 a share but they announced that they increased their Authorized Shares to 10 billion. So The Student promptly removed his bid and for good reason. The stock currently closed at $0.0009, down more than 50% from its day's high of $0.002 a share. Pay attention to the news!

He has also caught a few blue chip stocks as their charts formed perfect buy opportunities. The markets are way over bought at the moment. So he only considered stocks with prices that were below their intrinsic value and charts that passed his litmus test. One such stock was TEVA.

TEVA had a chart that showed the 10 day moving average crossing up through the 50 day moving average. And it was trading at $55.00 a share, well below its $77.00 a share intrinsic value, calculated through BuffetsBooks.com. Zack's also had a #2 buy rating on TEVA and the news was all positive. So the Student purchased shares of TEVA at $55.00. I'm not going to tell you where the price hit, you can look that up on StockCharts.com or your favorite stock charting website. But I'd advise you to do so.

All the Student wanted with his trades was 20%. However, the Student had to break even on AAPL. AAPL had an intrinsic value of $250.00 a share and is trading at below $150.00. But the shares of Apple are so heavily manipulated by traders that it will most likely never hit its intrinsic value. The Student is learning all of the time.

He bought AAPL at $128.00 a share and sold at $130.00 a share after he had received the dividend, of course. So he took a miniscule loss on AAPL. And speaking of the dividend, the Student did not sell all of his TEVA either. And he just received another dividend payment from them.

Currently the Student is eyeing KORS. They reported a negative revenue outlook from their quarterly report. And the price took a beaten because of it. But these are just projections and no one can predict the true financial numbers.

The KORS stock price had a major gap down and is currently trading at an unduly low price as of June 2015. Its intrinsic value is around $70.00 a share but is trading at below $50.00. If the price jumps back up to where it was before the news came out, $61.00 a share, those who buy these low prices will be sitting on an increase of roughly 22% which is about right where the Student wants his profit (20%). But remember to wait for the chart to completely bottom and to show a reversal pattern before buying a ticker.

Stock trading is not an exact science. It is an art. And if a trader works hard enough to become outstanding at the art of bottom feeding, he or she will reap the rewards that their sowed seeds of hours and hours of studying and reading will afford them.

Practice does not make perfect. Perfect practice makes perfect and warrants a smile of success that the author hopes you, as the reader and student of penny stocks, enjoy as the profits start rolling in.

Author

Have questions for the Author?

Connect with him on Twitter: @AuthJB

If you enjoyed this book and have found value in it, please help me out by leaving feedback on the website from which you purchased it. A positive review would be greatly appreciated. It's quick, easy, and extremely helpful. Thank you and good luck with your trading.

Books by Joseph Bronner:

Kamatia: The 2nd Age and the Legend of Krahm (Published: 2013)

The Anti-Anxiety Magic Book (Published: 2013)

The Anti-Anxiety Magic Book, the action book (Published: 2013)

Penny Stock Players (Published: 2014)

Penny Stock Players: Market Manipulation (Published: 2015)

Penny Stock Players: The Art of Bottom Feeding (Published: 2015)

Kamatia: The 1st Age and the Legend of Daegrom (Coming Soon)

Money Machine (Coming soon)

51242646R00100

Made in the USA
San Bernardino, CA
16 July 2017